THE REAL READER'S QU[ARTERLY]

Slightly Foxed

'Laughter in the Library'

NO.77 SPRING 2023

Editors: Gail Pirkis & Hazel Wood
Marketing & publicity: Steph Allen, Jennie Harrison Bunning & Hattie Summers
Subscriptions, orders & bookshops: Jess Dalby

Cover illustration: David Martin, *Spring Vase*

It was only after retirement from teaching art that David Martin (1922–2018) found success as a painter. Fortunately, ahead of him lay another 35 years devoted to painting and to establishing a distinctive approach that drew on his training at the Glasgow School of Art as well as his later interest in textile design. Through solo exhibitions in London, he established a considerable international following. He was a meticulous painter: nothing was left on the canvas that was extraneous or haphazard. Each element in the composition had to carry a clear purpose, and each colour was used as the visual tinder that would ignite an adjacent passage of paint. For more of his work visit the John Martin Gallery at www.jmlondon.com.

Back cover fox by James Nunn
Design by Octavius Murray
Layout by Andrew Evans
Colophon and tailpiece by David Eccles

© The contributors 2023

Published by Slightly Foxed Limited
53 Hoxton Square
London N1 6PB

tel 020 7033 0258
email office@foxedquarterly.com
www.foxedquarterly.com

Slightly Foxed is published quarterly in early March, June, September and December

Annual subscription rates (4 issues)
UK and Ireland £56; Overseas £64

Single copies of this issue can be bought for £14.50 (UK) or £16.50 (Overseas)

All back issues in printed form are also available

ISBN 978-1-910898-78-9

ISSN 1742-5794

Printed and bound by Smith Settle, Yeadon, West Yorkshire

Contents

Contents

Isla Middleton

From the Editors

There's something very particular about the quiet months after Christmas – a time to hibernate, turn round and generally take stock. That's what we've been doing here at the Slightly Foxed office, tidying up after the Christmas rush, reviewing our plans for the coming year and watching spring gradually arrive in Hoxton Square as the daffodils begin to emerge and the cafés tentatively put out their tables.

A little book we've just published beautifully captures the essence of the season. *A Countryman's Spring Notebook* brings together more of the popular weekly essays Adrian Bell contributed for thirty years to the *Eastern Daily Press*, each one a fleeting moment evoked with a painterly eye and the down-to-earth observation of the farmer Bell became. A must for all those who've come to love his writing and one to put alongside *A Countryman's Winter Notebook* which we published last year.

Our new Slightly Foxed Edition is something very different. In *True to Both My Selves* (see p.11) Katrin FitzHerbert tells the unusual story of her family, and of growing up as the child of a half-English mother and a German father, a man she idolized who was a committed member of the Nazi Party. With great courage and honesty she describes how she moved from a childhood dedicated to the ideals of National Socialism to face her past and make the final choice 'between England and Papa'.

When Dame Hilary Mantel died, many readers of her novels learned more about her life and her heroic struggle with the serious medical condition from which she suffered for many years without a diagnosis. Nowhere is this more vividly or more movingly described than in her own memoir *Giving Up the Ghost*, which is now available in a Plain Foxed Edition. It's the story of the painful making of a great writer, a story not easy to forget.

This was the 14th year of our popular crossword competition. Congratulations to the winner, Jonathan Crowther in Oxford, who receives a free annual subscription. For any of you still foxed, the answers are on p.94.

And finally the sentence we wish we didn't have to write: as from this issue the price of an annual subscription is going up by £8 (or less than the cost of a coffee per issue, if that feels any better!). We've managed to hold it steady for the past four years, and those of you who've been with us for a while will know that *SF* is never going to make us rich, and that we're not out for the last penny. However, the costs of producing the magazine have rocketed to the point where, rather than compromise on quality, we feel we have no option but to raise the price.

We do understand that your costs must have rocketed too, but we hope you'll stick with us if you possibly can and still feel you're getting your money's worth, which does include book discounts, our newsletters, podcasts and free access to all the articles in our online archive, plus the comfort and cheer that *SF* seems to bring – and when was that ever more needed?

GAIL PIRKIS & HAZEL WOOD

The Slightly Foxed Podcast
A new episode of our podcast is available on the 15th of April, July, October and January. To listen, visit www.foxedquarterly.com/pod or search for Slightly Foxed on Audioboom, Apple Podcasts or your podcast app.

Subscriber Benefits
Slightly Foxed can obtain any books reviewed in this issue, whether new or second-hand. To enquire about a book, access the digital edition of *Slightly Foxed* or view a list of membership benefits, visit www.foxedquarterly.com/members or contact the office: 020 7033 0258/office@foxedquarterly.com.

Laughter in the Library

MARTIN SORRELL

When, on what felt like my 800th lockdown circuit of the park, I came across a fellow-walker trying his damndest to stop his dog barking at something unseen among the trees and get it on the move again, suddenly the name Dogmatix popped into my mind, remembered from Anthea Bell's marvellous English translations of the *Asterix* comic-strip stories written by René Goscinny and illustrated by Albert Uderzo.

I left the dog and his master to it, and as I pushed on round my three miles, to exercise my brain I started thinking up names ending in 'ix' to add to those which Ms Bell had fashioned as Anglo-Saxon matches for Goscinny's Gallic originals. It was a welcome mental workout, and good fun, a game of the kind they play on radio's dottiest comedy, *I'm Sorry I Haven't a Clue*. New names kept coming, one every few paces. Predictably, Prefix and Suffix came first; then feline Catatonix, flamboyant Histrionix, thespian manqué Amateur-dramatix. And on it went until Pandemix stole in and I put a stop to the game.

For those of us – can there be many? – who haven't discovered Asterix for ourselves or through our children, let me introduce him and his world. The year is 50 BC. Gaul has been entirely overrun by the Romans except for one village at the top left of the country, holding out even though encircled by the fortified camps of

All 38 of René Goscinny and Albert Uderzo's *Asterix* books are available in paperback from Orion.

Laudanum, Compendium, Totorum and Aquarium. Diminutive, bulbous-nosed Asterix, sporting a Mercury-winged helmet and a moustache like two haystacks (haystax, even), doesn't look cut from the cloth of heroes. He is, however, possessed of superhuman strength thanks to regular swigs of a magic potion brewed from mistletoe and worse by the resident druid Getafix.

Asterix's bosom friend and companion-in-arms is Obelix, a giant who by trade is – wonderfully inspired invention, this – a menhir delivery man. Good-natured, simple-minded and seriously obese, Obelix is also possessed of impossible strength, though unlike Asterix and everyone else, he never needs to top it up with potion since he ingested a lifetime's supply when as a baby he fell into the druid's vat. What Obelix *does* need, however, is to consume at least one boar a day. He's the owner of Dogmatix, a sensitive little terrier who howls in empathetic anguish every time a tree is felled.

Then there's Vitalstatistix, the village chief who has no fears other than that the sky will fall on him tomorrow, which of course won't happen since, as everyone knows, tomorrow never comes. Last but – to the detriment of everyone's eardrums – not least, there's Cacofonix the bard, a self-proclaimed genius who's universally loved and admired so long as he doesn't speak and especially doesn't sing.

Goscinny's inspiration for Asterix was Vercingetorix, chief of the Arverni tribe, who, towards the end of Julius Caesar's Gallic Wars, united what remained of Gaul's tribes in an uprising against the Roman occupiers. In 52 BC, under Vercingetorix's leadership, the Gauls won a famous victory at Gergovia, a long way from Asterix's Brittany – it's near today's Clermont-Ferrand – but shortly after they were defeated at the Battle of Alesia, in Burgundy. To safeguard the lives of his surviving troops, Vercingetorix gave himself up and was carted off to Rome where five years later he was publicly executed. His surrender to Julius Caesar was depicted by the late nine-teenth-century artist Lionel Royer. The moustache he's given Vercingetorix, a curving auburn flourish, suggests to me not so much a Gaul as a Royal Air Force wing commander; nor do his fine-boned and chiselled features make him look like the native of Auvergne that he was. I should know. The faces of my Auvergnat great-uncles and second cousins were scarcely models of refinement; and, like ninety-nine per cent of adult males in the southern parts of France, their moustaches were as black and uncurated as a house-painter's brush.

As soon as the pandemic eased enough to let my town's library re-open, I made my way to its children's section, where over thirty titles in the *Asterix* series are shelved. I skimmed the pages inside whichever of Uderzo's lively covers appealed most. To reset the scene, I looked particularly at the first title in the series, *Asterix the Gaul* (1961). Then I proceeded to no. 8, *Asterix in Britain* (1966), and took it out on loan. I was intrigued to see what Goscinny had made of the goings-on among the *rosbifs* of Albion.

The plot didn't matter too much: Asterix and Co. bring a vat of the magic potion across the Channel to assist chief Mykingdomforanos and his fighters in the last village still resisting the Romans. Battle ensues, but the Romans – Stratocumulus, Claudius Detritus, Encyclopaedia Britannicus et al. – fail to get hold of the potion. A great victory for the village, but frankly it's surprising the Brits can prevail in *any* battle, let alone this one, given their custom of disen-gaging from hostilities at five o'clock sharp to drink hot water with a spot of milk. Nor will they countenance fighting at weekends, when they like to gather in The Jolly Boar and The Jug and Amphora for warm beer and chat punctuated by 'old fruit', 'old chap', 'jolly good show', 'I say' and other expressions beyond any Gaul's understand-ing. I'd expected there to be a gentlemanly game of cricket at some point; instead, we get a rugby match of unspeakable ferocity, the teams cheered on by the crowd's 'Hipiphurrax! Hipiphurrax!'

I finished *Asterix in Britain* musing on what Goscinny and Uderzo would have concocted had they produced a mirror story of the Brits in Gaul, *Mykingdomforanos in Brittany*, say. It would surely have been larded with clichés about the French, who'd be off to war in Citroën 2CVs, wearing berets, chewing garlic, smoking Gauloises and necking *vin rouge*, accompanied by wives and mistresses and chihuahuas in body-warmers. Battle would have been suspended on the stroke of midday for two-hour lunches of frogs' legs and snails. And someone somewhere would have had an aunt with a plume . . .

Yet, despite the fun and fantasy, I couldn't rid my thoughts of Pandemix, that grisly interloper who set me thinking about the backcloth to *Asterix*. Goscinny's idea for the series germinated in the 1950s, when the memory of the Second World War was still very raw and painful in France. Goscinny must have had in mind the enemy occupation of his country as he set about creating the Gaul of *Asterix*. For Caesar's Rome, read Nazi Germany; for Asterix and his fellow fighters, General de Gaulle, the Free French and the Resistance . . . And then, what about today? The pandemic, Ukraine? Does either have comic potential? Perhaps, when a new Goscinny and a new Uderzo arrive on the scene sometime in the future, the answer will be yes.

But enough of dark thoughts! Should any be lingering when I next visit the library, they'll evaporate the moment I turn to the first page of whichever of those large-format white-covered *Asterix* titles I next pull off the shelf. And if, rather than taking it home, I decide to settle down and read it straight through there and then, I'll be sure to stifle my laughter. Even in the relaxed atmosphere of libraries today, it wouldn't do to have hysterix.

Now that *Asterix* has won him over again, MARTIN SORRELL wants to dig out the *Tintin* stories he loved as a child to see if they too have retained their magic.

A Hybrid Life

ANTHONY WELLS

By the time she was 14 and finally settled with her family in their own house in Totnes, Devon, Katrin FitzHerbert – or Kay Norris, as she was then – had lived in nearly thirty different places and attended no fewer than fourteen schools. To have lived such an itinerant life by such a tender age would be extraordinary in itself but, to make her story even more unusual, the homes and schools were in two countries, Germany and England. And there was a further complication. The Germany where she spent the first years of her life, moving from place to place and school to school, was the Germany of the Third Reich, the Second World War and the Allied occupation. For Katrin FitzHerbert, the author of *True to Both My Selves* (1997), was born Katrin Olga Ethel Thiele in Berlin on 6 June 1936.

Her story, however, begins neither in Germany nor with Katrin, but in London, in the first years of the twentieth century, with her maternal grandparents. As her book's subtitle *A Family Memoir of Germany and England in Two World Wars* indicates, Katrin is not the only person with whom the story is concerned or, indeed, the only person who tells it; through the letters and reminiscences of other family members she is able to widen the scope of her book and its narration beyond her own direct experience.

No figure contributes more to this than her grandmother Ethel, known throughout the book not as Grandma, but its German version, Oma. The counterpart for Grandpa is Opa and it is with the 1905 marriage of the expatriate Richard Druhm to the London-born Ethel Norris that this tangled Anglo-German family saga begins.

We British are accustomed in the history of Anglo-German relations to take the moral high ground, but the circumstances in which Katrin's Oma and Opa find themselves in 1919, with an 8-year-old English daughter in tow, being deported as enemy aliens and forced to start a new life in Germany, are part of an ugly, and still not widely known, xenophobic episode in British history. Suffice to say that during the First World War the law-abiding, inoffensive, 50,000-strong German minority in London were so ill-treated by both the British government and the British public that Grandma Ethel had few regrets in deciding to follow her cruelly expelled husband back to his German homeland. Settling in the small town of Köpenick on the outskirts of Berlin, and – in stark contrast to the way they had been made to feel in London – given a warm reception by the locals, Richard and Ethel set about laying the foundations of a new family existence in Germany, as Germans, that would last just short of thirty years.

This was how the author of *True to Both My Selves* came to be born in Germany and how the first of her two selves, the German one, came into being. Her mother Elfreda – so named, back in London in 1910, to allow for both English (Freda) and German (Elfi) variants – adapted readily to her new homeland. Despite knowing no German before arriving in the country, she made a success of her schooling and quickly found work in the publicity section of one of Berlin's leading department stores.

By 1931, at the age of 21, she had also fallen in love and married a German man, a step which meant finally changing her nationality and becoming German. Two years later the couple's first child, Udo, was born, followed three years later by Katrin. It was now 1936, and Adolf Hitler had been in power for three years. Katrin was born into a fully fledged National Socialist state, the character, atmosphere and ethos of which would impress themselves indelibly on the malleable personality of the little girl.

In all the voluminous literature about the Third Reich, it's rare to come across personal accounts that tell, as it were, the other side of the story. In some respects, of course, there is no other side to tell. But it is easy to close our eyes to the fact that, despite its ruthless rejection of democracy and individual freedom, National Socialism generated its own form of idealism, one which, by embracing traditional values dear to the German heart, appealed to large swathes of the population, not least the young. With extraordinary candour, the

Katrin and her brother Udo, Recklinghausen, 1945

adult author retraces the experiences and emotions of her 5- and 6-year-old self as she becomes an ardent member of the Nazi equivalent of the Brownies and enthusiastically embraces activities such as writing a letter to Hitler on his birthday and trooping off to a hayfield with hundreds of other children to help form a giant human swastika which, their teachers assured them, would delight the Führer on his flight-path east.

Key to the 6-year-old Katrin's growing attachment to the National Socialist creed is the fact that she loves her Papa, and her Papa is not just a committed Nazi but is employed by the Party as an official in the Hitler Youth. To 'Papa's little girl', as the author often refers to her former self, her father embodies all the noble virtues of the movement: the sense of duty, loyalty, obedience, of sacrifice of self to a greater cause. As a result, the story of how the maturing Katrin grapples with the Nazi-inspired beliefs of her past self – the real heart of her book – is closely interwoven with her painful attempts to free herself from her idolization of her father.

True to Both My Selves thus becomes, in its way, a model example of a process known to Germans from the late 1950s as *Vergangenheitsbewältigung*, best rendered in English as 'coming to terms with the past'. In German, this can apply both to individuals coming to terms, in a psychotherapeutic sense, with troubling events in their past and, more commonly, to postwar German society confronting the events, and specifically the crimes, of its Nazi predecessor. In doing the first, Katrin FitzHerbert's memoir cannot avoid – and does not seek to avoid – doing the second. It is this which drew praise from readers such as James Callaghan and Mary Wesley when the book was first published twenty-five years ago, the former prime minister admiring its 'honesty and integrity', Mary Wesley describing it simply as 'a very brave book, it should be read by all generations' – judgements with which new readers of *True to Both My Selves* will, I'm certain, find themselves in agreement.

The first of the author's two selves is that of the girl raised in Germany's Third Reich; the second is that of her English successor, Kay Norris, brought to England in 1946 by her mother, and expected, implicitly if not explicitly, to forget entirely about the first. Before the family reaches English shores, however, the reader is taken, courtesy of Oma and Opa, on a gripping journey through the ruins and chaos of the collapsing Third Reich, through the frightening early stages of the Soviet occupation and then into the more easy-going order of the British-controlled region of western Germany. It is here that the family begin their metamorphosis back into their English selves and Katrin finds herself faced with an impossible dilemma: the 'straightforward choice', as she puts it, 'between England and Papa'. Ultimately she chooses England, her eye-opening experience of the 1950 General Election campaign having kindled a fascination with politics which makes her want to study the subject at university. Papa emigrates to

Canada with his new wife, and Katrin, burying her memories of him and her German past, embarks on her own adult life.

But the past, as William Faulkner observed, is 'never dead. It's not even past', a truth Katrin discovers for herself when, well into her fifties, she sets out to explore the history of her family and her 'two selves'. It is only when she clears up the mystery of her father's actions in the final days of the Second World War, and confronts the terrible record of the regime she was brought up to idolize, that she reaches some kind of accommodation, uneasy though it may be, with the two elements of her being. It is a fitting and moving conclusion to the voyage of moral discovery which is the ultimate significance of this courageous and skilfully constructed book.

For many years Nazi Germany, its history and ideology were at the centre of ANTHONY WELLS's working life, when he was a librarian at the Wiener Library in London (now the Wiener Holocaust Library). Though he had left before Katrin FitzHerbert visited, he was not surprised to find that she had made use of the Library's resources during her research for *True to Both My Selves*. You can also hear him in Episode 27 of our podcast, discussing Dr Wiener's Library.

Katrin FitzHerbert's *True to Both My Selves* (392pp) is now available in a limited and numbered cloth-bound edition of 2,000 copies (subscribers: UK & Eire £18, Overseas £20; non-subscribers £20, Overseas £22). All prices include post and packing. Copies may be ordered by post (53 Hoxton Square, London N1 6PB), by phone (020 7033 0258) or via our website www.foxedquarterly.com.

The Girl from Apex City

MARGARET DRABBLE

Edith Wharton's *The Custom of the Country* (1913) is one of the most sparkling and enjoyable novels I have ever read, and I've read it now several times. Each time it manages to surprise and delight me. I put it in a class with *Pride and Prejudice*, as a book that offers endlessly renewable pleasure. That's high praise, but I mean every word of it.

If it had any flaw – which it hasn't – it would be that of being *too* sparkling, a criticism that Austen herself acknowledged could be applied to her own work, wondering if readers might find her first novel 'rather too light and bright and sparkling'. All of Edith Wharton's books are enjoyable, but this one has an incomparably shining bravura. She must have been very pleased with it. It gives us a panorama of society at the height of the Belle Époque, in New York and Paris, with all the satisfactions of the classiest of costume dramas and the added reassurance that the novel isn't a facsimile: it is, as her friend Henry James would have put it, the Real Thing.

It is the story of Undine Spragg from the fictional Apex City in the Midwest (what a name, what a provenance!) and her relentless search for advancement. At the beginning we find her friendless and lonely, living in what she soon learns to be less than stylish affluence in a luxury hotel in New York with her lonely, wealthy and indulgent parents, whom she has bullied mercilessly since childhood. (The personalities of these, at first sight unpromising parents are developed with great subtlety.)

Edith Wharton, *The Custom of the Country* (1913)
OUP · Pb · 416pp · £8.99 · ISBN 9780199555123

Undine is a beauty, a head-turner, and she has set her sights on a society marriage. As we discover, although so evidently desirable, she is not very interested in sex, but she is seriously interested in fun. She likes fine clothes, jewels, expensive restaurants, dinner parties and any settings that will display her charms to the world. She likes to be where the action is, and we watch her as she continues to revise her opinion of where that might be. Although not conventionally intelligent (she has no interest in books or art, although she likes the chic world of the artist's studio) she is very smart, and very quick at picking up hints about the customs of the countries that she finds she wishes to conquer.

Wharton's title indicates her lively interest in anthropology. It is taken from a 1647 Jacobean drama by Fletcher and Massinger, referring to the feudal *droit de seigneur*, but Wharton uses the phrase to invoke in part the inbred manners of old New York, of which she gives an explicitly anthropological analysis: 'the Dagonet attitude, the Dagonet way of life, the very lines of furniture in the old Dagonet house' are likened to

> the Aborigines . . . these vanishing denizens of the American continent doomed to rapid extinction with the advance of the invading race. [Ralph] was fond of describing Washington Square as the 'Reservation', and of prophesying that before long its inhabitants would be exhibited at ethnological shows, pathetically engaged in the exercise of their primitive industries.

But she also focuses her attention on the emergent world, and on the complex and changing customs of the moneyed marriage market. In particular, she analyses the distinctions between the social status of American and European divorcées, distinctions which play a crucial role in the plot.

We watch Undine as she triumphantly trips her way through this minefield, deftly avoiding many a danger. The sensational plot is full of surprises, some of them with slow fuses, and some of them sprung upon us as sudden detonations: I had managed to forget the most shocking of all, so it came upon me this time round as a horrifying revelation. Wharton's handling of narrative is superb: her deft time breaks and swift cuts between chapter and chapter are a master class in pace and in the handling of expectation. She doesn't waste time on unnecessary linkages: she jumps, along with her heroine, to the next adventure, the next incarnation, the next unexpected marriage.

John Singer Sargent,
Lady Agnew of Lochnaw, 1892

Are we meant to admire the astonishing and shameless Undine? Clearly not: she is venal, apparently heartless, and a very bad mother. One of the most painful scenes in the book concerns her neglect of her only son Paul, whose birthday party she forgets under the heady influence of a glittering 'tea' held in honour of her newly painted portrait in the studio of Claud Walsingham Popple, a character inspired by John Singer Sargent (with maybe a touch of Whistler). Undine likes Popple, and she also likes his paintings: he is very good at pearls and fabrics, and all his sitters and their patrons ask of his portraits is that 'the costume should be sufficiently "life-like" and the face not too much so' – although in Undine's case, as Popple assures her, there has been no need to idealize: 'nature herself has outdone the artist's dream'. Surrounded by admirers and sycophants, she neglects to return home for her son's party, an event which precipitates the breakdown of her first society marriage and presages a life of uncertainty and sorrow and loneliness for Paul, who loses count of his fathers and grandparents as he is dragged, at her convenience, in her wake.

And yet, and yet. There is something primal in her energy, in her ambition, in her resolution. Wharton describes her as a 'pioneer', and the word has a powerful American resonance. One cannot wholly dislike her. The more we learn of her childhood in Apex, details of which are released slowly throughout the narrative, the more we come to feel a certain grudging admiration for her audacity, her contempt for conventional opinions, her willingness to carve her own fate.

The story of her developing relationship with her childhood beau from Apex, the self-made Elmer Moffatt, is full of nuance. He is the red-faced, overweight, ill-dressed, parentless boy from nowhere, who transforms himself into a Wall Street tycoon, a connoisseur of the arts and a great collector. He becomes a man who can look down on the works of Popple and his like. Undine, as a girl, had defied Apex by walking down Main Street on Moffatt's arm, when that small town with its small-town morality had turned against him because he had disgraced himself the night before at a temperance rally. The way she stuck by him at that moment has profound consequences for her, and for the society she moves in.

In the grand finale, we see her in Paris bedecked with pigeon-blood rubies that had once belonged to Marie Antoinette, but, like Alexander, she is still intent on conquest. She is still feeling 'that there were other things she might want if she knew about them'. Will she discover what they are? The novel was published in 1913, as the world was about to change forever, and so we cannot follow her illimitable desires beyond the great debacle.

MARGARET DRABBLE is a novelist and critic who is currently struggling to write a memoir. It began with an account of her mother's education and her admiration for George Gissing but has turned into a rambling covid lockdown memoir. Maybe she will sort it out and give it a shape one day. You can also hear her in Episode 17 of our podcast, discussing her writing life.

Waiting for Posterity

ROGER HUDSON

In 1786 Richard Wynne decided to sell his estate at Folkingham in Lincolnshire and go to live on the Continent with his wife and five daughters. The sale realized £90,000 and he had investments too; his wealth, eight figures in today's terms, meant he could lead as elaborate an existence as he wanted, and the hope was that his wife's health would be improved by living abroad. Moreover she was French, while his mother had been Italian and he had spent part of his youth in Venice, so perhaps it wasn't as radical a step as all that. Then his fifth daughter had been born in 1786, so he might have resigned himself to never having a male heir to inherit Folkingham.

For us the important thing is the obvious determination of the Wynnes that their daughters should be equipped with all the lady-like accomplishments, so the household included music, dancing and drawing masters as well as governesses and tutors. Among the good habits inculcated was diary-keeping and we find them beginning with this in August 1789, in Alsace, a little to the south of Strasbourg, ominously a month after the start of the French Revolution, when Betsey is 10 and Eugenia 9; Harriet's began later – she was then only 5. Their diaries record much dressing up and cross-dressing, card-playing, blind man's buff and frog-in-the-middle, visiting the neighbours, music-making and dancing (with and without music),

---

The Wynne Diaries, 1789–1820, were published by Oxford University Press in three volumes (1935, 1937 and 1940). A selection from them appeared in the World's Classics in 1952, and as an Oxford paperback in 1982. In 2007 *Travels in Two Sicilies* appeared: extracts from Betsey's diaries for the years 1817–20.

this often involving servants and peasants 'who stank terribly and were all a trifle tipsy', putting nettles down their father's secretary's bed, but also learning how to darn stockings and mend clothes. Their father meanwhile buys horses and goes shooting.

They move to Venice, where their eldest sister Mary has married an Italian, on the way enduring the bad roads and inns, broken axle trees, verminous beds and drunken postilions even wealthy travellers cannot avoid. In Venice the French ambassador, the Marquis de Bombelles, has been forced to resign rather than serve his new revolutionary masters and the two families agree to share a castle on the banks of Lake Constance in easternmost Switzerland. Here amateur dramatics and reading aloud from Molière, Racine or *Robinson Crusoe*, and learning German from Schiller's *Don Carlos* are added to the educational mix. A passing bassoonist is hired for Lent, and the girls sing at high mass but are allowed to skip the German sermon and have breakfast instead. Betsey dislikes the numbers of French émigrés arriving and the increasingly tiresome de Bombelles, who seems to hold her father in thrall: 'I would rather live in a cottage in England than among these proud Frenchmen.'

The massacre of the Swiss Guards in Paris in August 1792 makes all the French, whatever their politics, very unpopular with the local peasantry, who take the Wynnes to be French too. By early 1793, when Louis XVI is guillotined, Betsey records how she 'danced with the afflicted French this afternoon. Is there such another *drôle* nation?' In 1794 the Wynnes learn of the torture of their mother's parents by the sans-culottes at their home near Lyons. Later that year fear of the advancing revolutionary armies persuades Mr Wynne to go further east, alas with the de Bombelles in tow.

They move to Ratisbon (Regensburg), then still an enclave of the Holy Roman Empire and seat of its 'Perpetual Diet', within Bavaria on the Danube, essentially Protestant but with three Catholic bishops and three abbeys as well, all under the benign guidance of the Princess of Thurn and Taxis. Betsey is soon recruited by her to play at performances of the first act of *The Magic Flute* and the finale of *Don Giovanni* put on at her court. It is now, at the great age of 16, that Betsey expresses some shame and an accompanying very adult feeling of responsibility: 'It is very humiliating to see that all the women of Papa's family should have lost their character and that makes us more than anyone else be scrupulous for the least thing and keep up an irreproachable conduct.' She is referring here to her father's mother, Anna Gazzini from the Ionian island of Lefkas, procured for her Wynne grandfather by his gondolier according to the catty Lady Mary Wortley Montagu (see *SF* no.57) and only married by him some time after the birth of their first child, Giustiniana, who then acquired considerable notoriety for the number of her lovers, including Casanova. Giustiniana had married the Count von Rosenberg in 1761 but he had died in 1791 and now Betsey's aunt's last lover is one Benincasa, an ex-Jesuit. Finally there is her sister Mary, who seems to have fallen for her brother-in-law very shortly after her marriage. Now, 'She behaves herself every day worse. She has left Conegliano [her home] and has gone [off with] an *archiprête*, a man of bad reputation.'

At the end of 1795 de Bombelles' *valet de chambre* insults Mr Wynne's, who then knocks him down. According to Betsey the former is de Bombelles' 'darling, confidant and friend' and the only person who can 'arrange' his dozen false teeth. His master over-reacts, threatening to abuse Mr Wynne and so provoke a duel. When Wynne offers to give him satisfaction, he denies that he had wanted to fight. At last the Frenchman's hold over her father is ended and by March Betsey can rejoice that her family is on its way to Florence over the Brenner Pass. But soon they are fleeing from the French forces progressing rapidly down Italy, in the nick of time making it to Leghorn where Captain Thomas Fremantle of the frigate *Inconstant* takes them on board.

Thomas (b. 1765) has been in the Mediterranean for two years, often in the company of his good friend Nelson, distinguishing himself in March 1795 with his attack on the far larger French 84-gun *Ça Ira* during a major encounter with the French fleet, before Nelson then delivers the *coup de grâce*. From a sketchy diary he keeps it is plain that both he and Nelson, a married man, have a succession of 'dollies' as he calls them, or mistresses. In July 1795, when dining with Nelson on his ship, he remarks that 'He makes himself ridiculous with that woman', meaning Nelson's current mistress. Later he refers to one of his own, 'a Venetian dolly – ravenous bitch'. The day the Wynnes first come on board in June 1796 he notes that another called Adelaide comes off the *Inconstant* that very evening.

In spite of this, Thomas and Betsey feel drawn to each other from the start and by 12 July Betsey is recording how he acknowledged to her mother 'that he is partial to me, and as his fortune at present was not sufficient enough for him to maintain a family he said he should not keep us any longer with him'. The family are transferred to another ship while he sails off. When he sees them again in October the pace quickens once more, with Mrs Wynne offering him a marriage settlement of £5,000 with the promise of £10,000 on her husband's death. But by 30 December he is still dithering: 'Don't like the idea of parting with Madlle [his current dolly]. Get serious fits. [December 31] Amazingly attached to Betsey . . . I can't say I have on the whole behaved very well.' Only on 10 January are matters finally settled, as Eugenia bluntly records: 'Papa behaved very handsomely in granting him my sister and £8,000.' Two days later they are married, the event orchestrated by the glamorous ambassadress at Naples, Emma Hamilton, with George III's son Prince Augustus giving Betsey away and Queen Maria Carolina of Naples smoothing out any difficulties with the Catholic authorities.

Betsey sails off with her husband and harpsichord, immune it seems to seasickness, while he pursues prizes, including one laden with Joseph Bonaparte's furniture. There is also 'much flogging this morning which made Fremantle ill and broke my heart'. In July Nelson and he are involved in hand-to-hand fighting in small boats off Cadiz, of which Betsey does not approve: 'sacrificing men for nothing'. Later that month, in hopes of capturing Spanish treasure ships, a foolhardy night landing at Tenerife is attempted, in which Nelson loses his right arm and Fremantle has two musket balls through his. A pregnant Betsey nurses them as they sail back to England on Fremantle's ship.

His wound forces Fremantle to give up his command, Betsey has the first of her ten children, and they set up house in Buckinghamshire where he had been brought up. He takes up wood-turning and shoots his first partridge. They are at pains to maintain their friendship with the family of the Marquess of Buckingham, by far the grandest and richest of their neighbours. (In the 1800s the biggest of his sinecures, the Tellership of the Exchequer which he has held since he was 11, is making him between £20,000 and £25,000 a year.) He, a member of the great Grenville political dynasty, is the source of the patronage vital for advancing the career of an officer like Fremantle; luckily Fremantle's younger brother has for some time acted as a valuable political fixer for the Marquess, while the Marchioness and her daughter are Catholic like Betsey and her sisters.

Eugenia and Betsey have a regular immersion in the social swim each year during the London season, their musical skills much in demand. At home they have to make do with the Kettering Ball: 'a collection of tall, stout, immense women and not one good dancer. Few beaux and all parsons.' But things are very different each Christmas, spent at the Buckinghams' palatial Stowe, playing the new piano before the French royal family in exile or mixing with the Prince of Wales and Charles James Fox, attending the dinner given for 500 of the local poor or the feast for their children where they receive a shilling apiece and a baked potato.

Early in 1801 Betsey is forthright about Lady Nelson's separation and the emergence of what might be called England's first Celebrity Couple: 'I have no patience with her husband, at his age and such a cripple to play the fool with Lady Hamilton.' But soon Nelson is telling Fremantle, back at sea in command of the *Ganges*, that she must be next in line to his own ship in the desperate battle which is to be fought at Copenhagen. From this point on there are frequent extracts from Fremantle's letters to Betsey, telling her for instance about the tedium of being part of a blockading squadron, 'bile and ennui: I do nothing but take snuff and read Shakespeare when I am off the quarterdeck'. She in return tells him how two of their children have been introduced to Queen Charlotte by her daughter Princess Sophia.

Come October 1805 and Freemantle must put aside his pug dog, cat and monkey as Trafalgar looms: Nelson 'told me I should have my old place in the line of battle, which is his second'. There Fremantle's ship, the three-decker *Neptune*, takes the surrender of the four-decker *Santissima Trinidad* single-handed. It is another year before he is back in England, where he is suddenly the beneficiary of major patronage, appointed a Lord of the Admiralty in Buckingham's brother Lord Grenville's Ministry. But by March 1807 it has fallen, and three years go by before he is on the upward path again, promoted to Admiral and serving once more in the Mediterranean. By the time the war finally ends he has been off Toulon, at Minorca, Tunis, Vis off the Croatian coast and Trieste, freeing the entire Adriatic of the French, and has been made a Knight of the Bath. By his death at Naples in 1819 he is Commander-in-Chief in the Mediterranean and a Baron of the Austrian Empire. Betsey lives until 1857, and by then there are more than sixty volumes of her and Eugenia's diaries waiting for posterity.

Whenever there is a jam on the A1 and he diverts to the A15 through Folkingham, ROGER HUDSON thinks of Betsey Wynne, whom he first encountered on her honeymoon when doing a book on Nelson and Emma in 1994. For those who would like to read more about the Wynne family, Roger has supplied an appendix which can be found on our website: see www.foxedquarterly.com/roger-hudson-wynne-diaries.

Shock Treatment

SUE GEE

In the summer of 1971, I answered an ad in *Time Out*: a Hampstead couple required an evening cook. I am no cook, but I was living on very little and accordingly presented myself for interview at a house in Downshire Hill, considerably more elegant than the rambling old place where I was renting an attic.

The door was answered by a well-dressed, crisply spoken woman in her early forties, who introduced herself and showed me to a room I have never forgotten. Light and airy, with French windows, pictures and a vast mahogany dining-table, its entire floor was ankle-deep in screwed-up pieces of white paper. No mention was made of this, and I can remember only one remark. 'I think holidays are a waste of time, don't you? They take you away from your *work*.'

I did not get the job, and I'm glad, for I would have been wasting the time of an extraordinary, brilliant and eventually mysterious writer for whom every hour was precious. It was only decades afterwards that I discovered who she was. Browsing in Philip Larkin's *Oxford Book of Twentieth Century English Verse*, I came upon 'Story of a Hotel Room' in which an illicit few hours – gloomy light, shutters with an awkward hook – lead to the danger of profound and unexpected love.

> Thinking we were safe – insanity! . . .
> To make love as well as that is ruinous.

Rosemary Tonks, *Bedouin of the London Evening: Collected Poems and Selected Prose*, with an introduction by Neil Astley (second enlarged edition, 2016) · Bloodaxe Books · Pb · 160pp · £12.99 · ISBN 9781780373614: *The Bloater* (1968) · Vintage · Pb · 142pp · £8.99 · ISBN 9781784877804

I don't know how I made the connection with those snowy heaps of discarded drafts but, captivated by the poem and seeing the author's name, I suddenly realized: Rosemary Tonks! That was *her*. But by this time, as I sought to find out more about her, she had long since disappeared. No one knew why, and nobody knew where she was. For a long time, many thought she was dead.

Born in 1928, Rosemary Tonks, whom a few surviving photographs show as a strikingly beautiful young woman, was the author of two volumes of poetry, *Notes on Cafés and Bedrooms* (1963) and *Iliad of Broken Sentences* (1967). 'Epoch-making' is how her most recent publisher has described them. The Bodley Head jacket note to the second collection introduces poems in which: 'The deserts of the Middle East are again equated with city life . . . its sofas, hotel corridors, cinemas, underworlds, cardboard suitcases . . . its anguish, its enraged excitement, its great lonely joys.'

'The main duty of the poet is to excite, to send the senses reeling,' Tonks once said, and her sensuous, jazzy, declamatory, urgent verses – 'hyper-urban, angst-ridden' as one critic described them – spattered with exclamation marks, are filled with startling imagery and startling disclosures.

> We move arrogantly into one another's power,
> And the last barriers go down between us . . .
> My refrigerated body feels the coffin's touch in every word
> You utter, and backs away for ever from your bed.
> 'The Drinkers of Coffee', 1967

'My ethos is a great European Metropolis,' she said. 'I want to show human passions at work and to give eternal forces their contemporary dimension in this landscape.' In 'Orpheus in Soho' these ideas find unforgettable expression, turning nightclubs, bars and alleys into the furnishings of Hades, while 'the brim of the world is lit, and breath pours softly over the Earth . . .'

Tonks was also the author of six sharp, autobiographical novels, published over seven years, whose titles are as arresting as the poetry collections: *Opium Fogs* (1963), *The Bloater* (1968), *Businessmen as Lovers* (1969), *The Way out of Berkeley Square* (1970). You might call one or two mannered and brittle, but the prose in all of them sparkles, skewering pretension, sex and everyday life with a wit and accuracy which have echoes of Oscar Wilde, Muriel Spark, Evelyn Waugh. They were written in a period of extraordinary productivity. Between 1963 and 1974, when she wrote a fine essay on Colette, Rosemary Tonks produced the poetry collections, the novels and some unflinching reviews for leading journals. With the BBC Radiophonic Workshop, she also took part in a very Sixties experimental poetry-and-sound event, *Sono-Montage*, broadcast in 1966. She was a friend of Edith Sitwell, admired by Cyril Connolly and John Wain, gave interviews.

But in 1968 a tragedy slowly unleashed a long, unstoppable descent into despair. This was the death of her mother, Thea, in a shocking accident. They had had a particularly difficult start to their relationship: Rosemary's businessman father died in Africa before she was born, and she spent time in foster homes, before being sent to a boarding-school in Bournemouth from which she was expelled at 16.

> In the green rags of the Bible I tore up
> The straight silk of childhood on my head
> I left the house, I fled
> My mother's brow where I had no ambition
> But to stroke the writing
> I raked in.

This passionate, prophetic poem, 'Running Away' (1963), delineates a real tension between mother and daughter, yet they were very close. Like fragile Thea, who married again but whose second husband also died in Africa, Rosemary came to believe in mediums and a spirit world – something which she later felt had done her great harm. And in Thea's second widowhood, on their return from Lagos to London, they lived together in poverty. It was then, aged 18, that Rosemary began to read deeply and seriously, discovering Baudelaire – like Rimbaud, a lasting influence – while hanging out in Soho.

Within two years she was married: to Mickey Lightband, six years older, and another businessman whose work took him much abroad. In Karachi she contracted polio, and for the rest of her life wore a stylish black glove to conceal her withered right hand – she taught herself to write with her left. And in 1954, when they settled down in Hampstead, a life began which combined intense work with memorable dinner parties. At these she shone. Family members recall how funny she was, how generous, and how much the centre of attention. At some point during these years, an aunt gave her a collection of Oriental treasures – god-figures from China and the Far East – to be held in trust.

This creative, vivid, fêted life began to break apart with her mother's death. She continued to write, but over the course of eight years she embarked on a spiritual quest, turning her back on the Christianity of her childhood, attending spiritualist meetings, consulting mediums and healers. Was she seeking to reconnect with the mother by whom, as a fostered only child, she had felt abandoned?

Her marriage ended. Living alone – not far from Mickey, who had a new wife and whom she never forgave – she was plagued by neuritis in her writing arm and serious eye-problems. To deal with these she began a punishing routine of Daoist eye exercises and meditation which ended in an emergency operation and left her almost blind. Further disasters included a burglary and a hopeless lawsuit. By 1977, describing herself as 'psychologically smashed', she rarely left the house.

By the following year she had left London, telling no one outside the family where she had gone. 'My life, my work, my hopes!' she had written in 'Rome' (1963), another prophetic line. All, it seemed, had gone from her now, her life itself a broken sentence. In 1980 she sold the house in Downshire Hill and locked the Oriental collection in the bank: she had begun to fear those graven images, and with a sense of revelation she returned to the Bible. This became the one true book, and she never opened another.

And in 1981 she withdrew the 'heathen' gods and smashed them to smithereens. She had been working on a novel about a man's search for God. She burned it all to ash. 'I can tell you I meant business,' she later told her great-niece in a letter. The fury and passion with which she did all this is there in many of her poems: 'Badly Chosen Lover', 'Done For', 'Fog Peacocks', 'I May Destroy You', 'Running Away'. Now she had run away with a vengeance, the door on the world slammed shut.

I would say that her spirit was broken, save that a new spiritual life was about to begin. That year she travelled to Jerusalem and was baptised in the River Jordan. This, she wrote, was her 'second birth'. And although she never wrote another line of poetry, she continued to write: letters to her family, though she never saw them, and in countless notebooks.

In 2009 Brian Patten presented a BBC Radio 4 programme en-titled 'The Vanished Poet'. Was Rosemary Tonks hiding in some smoky European city, so vividly realized in much of her work? Had she taken up residence in a souk, or a tent in the desert, again a repeated theme? Had she died?

It was Neil Astley, publisher of Bloodaxe Books, who told Patten that she was alive but, sworn to secrecy by her family, he did not reveal her whereabouts. She was living in Bournemouth, taken in by her kindly maternal aunt in 1978 and comforted back to health. From her house Rosemary had moved to a secluded one not far away, where she drew the curtains, refused to answer the phone, regarded postcards from Astley as communications from Satan, and lived as Mrs Rosemary Lightband until her death, in 2014, at the age of 85.

She became one of those people who creep into church and out again, speaking to no one; who give out bibles at Speakers' Corner, and have just a single friend, who knows nothing about them. She is buried in the Church of St Thomas à Becket, in Hampshire, in her mother's grave.

She has gone, but she haunts the modern mind. It is Neil Astley who has brought her back into print, introducing her to a new generation with *Bedouin of the London Evening: Collected Poems* in 2014. Within the last couple of years at least three references have appeared in novels and radio programmes and at least one young poet, Lizzie Palmer, has embraced her idiom. You can hear her on a podcast from the British Library, where you can also hear Rosemary herself, reading in her cut-glass voice poems from her old, unbroken life: poems which with every line say, 'Hear me!'

SUE GEE's novel *Earth and Heaven* (2000), set at the Slade School of Art between the wars, features Henry Tonks, surgeon and Professor of Painting, and Rosemary's great-uncle. You can also hear her in Episode 3 of our podcast, discussing the art of editing.

The River and Its Source

JIM CRUMLEY

There are two memorials to Neil Gunn in his birthplace of Dunbeath on the Caithness coast. One is a statue and the other is a squat black typewriter. The typewriter is a mid-1930s Imperial. I have never much cared for the concept of sacred relics, but if pushed I could make a case for that typewriter. It was the one on which Gunn wrote *Highland River* (1937), a novel so exquisitely wrought that it conferred on his native landscape the gift of immortality.

The statue is not what you might expect: not Gunn himself but a boy with a huge salmon in his arms. This is Kenn, the central character of *Highland River*, and the salmon is the thirty-pounder he poached with his bare hands as a 9-year-old boy. So what the statue commemorates is a moment in fiction that consumes the book's first sixteen pages, and if there is a finer opening to any book anywhere in Scotland's literature of the land, I have never heard of it. The first chapter of *Highland River* stands alone.

If on your travels you should ever chance on Dunbeath, the guardians of the reputation of their village's most famous son would like you to appreciate the significance of where you stand. Hence the statue, not of the most famous son himself, but rather the fruits of his finest hour. Everything I have ever written that is any good at all began life with a landscape, the book's bedrock. Whenever I have wavered in the tricky art of writing down a particular portion of the surface of planet Earth so that it gives the book I am trying to write

Neil Gunn, *Highland River* (1937)
Canongate · Pb · 256p · £9.99 · ISBN 9781782118848

its sure foundation, I renew my conviction by revisiting *Highland River*, because it is the apotheosis of that art.

It must be forty years since our paths first crossed, although I can no longer remember the moment. It wasn't the first Gunn novel I'd read but it caused me to elevate him into the ranks of the immortals. *The Silver Darlings* (see *SF* no. 45) has won many more plaudits, but I think *Highland River* belongs to a higher order, one of the masterworks of Scottish literature.

Neil Gunn

What I do remember is that about twenty years ago, while I was doing some work with the Caithness-based publisher Keith Whittles, I gave a talk in Dunbeath's Neil Gunn Centre and without any warning, and with a startling surge of emotion akin to an electric shock, I came face to face with that typewriter. It was like being handed Robert Burns's quill or Louis Armstrong's trumpet or Toscanini's baton. It had a repair label attached with the date 1937, the year *Highland River* was published. So these were the very keys that typed:

Out of that noiseless world in the grey of the morning, all his ancestors came at him. They tapped his breast until the bird inside it fluttered madly; they drew a hand along his hair until the scalp crinkled; they made the blood within him tingle to a dance that had him leaping from boulder to boulder before he rightly knew to what desperate venture he was committed.

For it was all in a way a sort of madness . . . A thousand

influences had his young body taut as a bow, when at last, bending over a boulder of the old red sandstone, he saw again the salmon.

The river, unnamed in the book, is the Dunbeath Water, an artery of lifeblood that flowed through Gunn's young life. Its source lies in the wild but unsung back-country of Caithness, and it binds the source both to the sea and to the lives of centuries of sea-thirled villagers. It laves the salt-smitten walls and waters of their very harbour with its high-moor sweetness, tempering the harshness of their place on the map of the world, softening the natural brutality of the coast.

Strength was the keynote of this coast, a passionless remorseless strength, unyielding as the rock, tireless as the water; the unheeding rock that a falling body would smash itself to pulp upon; the transparent water that would suffocate an exhausted body in the slow rhythm of its swirl. There was a purity about it all, stainless as the gull's plumage, wild and cold as its eye.

Highland River is a book about belonging, about a sense of place, about how we are shaped by landscape. The first of all our landscapes never leaves us, and wherever life may lead us, we never truly leave that first landscape. The child that absorbs that nursery landscape by osmosis and without questioning it lives on in our adult selves, and it is only as adults that we begin to question who we are and where we belong.

Kenn's life began 'where the river was lost in the sea', but his individuality emerged as he began to explore upstream, towards the source. And that, in a nutshell, is Gunn's plot. The novel slides backwards and forwards in time through eighteen years of Kenn's life from the day of the salmon through adolescence and university to being gassed in the trenches of the First World War to a glimpse of the mature 37-year-old nuclear physicist. Through it all, his heart and mind are forever drawing on the essence of that childhood, forever embedded in the strath that nurtured it, the strath and its river: 'It is a lovely strath . . . It is not a glen of the mountains, craggy, stupendous, physically impressive. There is nothing here to overwhelm the romantic mind. Its beauty is an inward grace in oneself akin to what is indefinable in the memory of a masterpiece.'

Slowly, and with deft subtlety, Gunn insinuates the book's inner theme, a quest to discover the source, a lifelong journey that explores the physical landscape all the way to the source of the river and an inner journey in which Kenn unearths the source of himself. It is a journey fashioned from three elements: his human ancestry (a potent mix of Norse, Gael and Pict, and back beyond that to who knows?), and the very land itself. The third element is nature, those creatures that populate it, and to which Gunn often ascribes eerie symbolism, as though all nature had a double meaning:

> The cry of the peewit is the cry of the living human, anxious, swift, flashing to earth. The long cry of the curlew passes overhead, disembodied and unearthly. Once the crying of curlews in the night had made him think of the men and women and children burned out of their homes in Strathnaver more than a century before. The spirits of his people, the disinherited, the nameless, the folk.

And then there is this startling echo during a conversation the 37-year-old Kenn has with his scientific colleague in the laboratory they share:

> Radzyn looked narrowly at him, at the smiling, unwavering eyes, and saw deep in the eyes the indissoluble hard core, the native, inalienable residium, saw it with the surprise one might come upon on a face in a mirror or a still adder-head in a pleasant bunch of heather.

What an image!

Highland River then, is part fiction, part nature writing. The plot is elusive, almost abstract at times, but as a nature writer myself it delights me. Gunn's constant interleaving of humankind, wildlife and the land, and the land with the sea through the river and the land-rooted, sea-thirled people's story . . . all that creates the sense of a single indivisible life force in which there is no distance between any of its constituent parts, and their interdependence is as manifest as it is beautiful.

If there is to be any hope at all for our troubled planet and humankind's place on it, it can only be realized by shrinking the wholly artificial distance that we as a species have put between ourselves and what we like to call 'the natural world'. But there is no natural world, there is only the world, and the unnatural regime our species insists upon. There is only nature, there isn't anything else. Neil Gunn knew that more than eighty years ago and articulated it in *Highland River*.

At the end of the book, the adult Kenn returns to the river after an absence of years following the death of his parents, and Gunn finally spells out the nature of the quest for the source, 'to provide the core of life with warmth and light'.

> Out of great works of art, out of great writing, there comes upon the soul sometimes a feeling of strange intimacy. It is the moment in which all conflict is resolved, in which a timeless harmony is achieved. It was coming upon him now.

> We should put up a statue to that.

JIM CRUMLEY was born in Dundee on the banks of the Firth of Tay, where he enjoyed a childhood steeped in nature. The final volume of his tetralogy of the seasons, *The Nature of Summer,* was published in 2020. You can also hear him in Episode 25 of our podcast, discussing literary landscapes.

The Consequences of War

MIRANDA SEYMOUR

A couple of years ago, a publisher sent me a pre-publication copy of a novel by Georgina Harding. I'm so glad she did for otherwise I might never have come across the work of an outstanding writer, one who deserves a much wider audience.

'There are images that stay like stains on the memory,' remarks Jonathan Ashe early on in *The Gun Room* (2016), the first book in Georgina Harding's marvellous *Harvest* trilogy. Intentionally or not, he's paraphrasing the photographer Diane Arbus, whose actual words provide the epigraph to the trilogy, alerting readers to the novelist's theme: '[Photographs] are the proof of something that was there and no longer is. Like a stain.'

It seems at first as if Jonathan's observation relates only to the Vietnam War photograph that has made him famous, not of the dead mother he saw lying on a path – a Vietnamese farm girl gunned down as she walked with her hoe to the fields – but that of the American soldier who sat alone in the dust by a nearby village wall, seen but unseeing. Later, by almost too neat a coincidence, the photographer again encounters his subject, now a handsome civilian adrift in Tokyo, where both men are seeking in anonymity some refuge from their damaged pasts.

Jonathan had grown up in England, on a tranquil family farm in Norfolk. The soldier, Jim, is a pastor's son, bred on the flat farmlands of Iowa. But it isn't simply a shared rural background that connects

Georgina Harding's *The Gun Room* (2016), *Land of the Living* (2018) and *Harvest* (2021) are all available as Bloomsbury paperbacks.

the pair. 'You took that picture,' Jim states, before accusing Jonathan of 'sightseeing' in a world he knows nothing about:

> People see your pictures and say, yeah, that's war. They have these words to go with the pictures. That's a soldier in a war. They think they know what the soldier did . . . They think they know, and they know nothing.

Talking to his Japanese girlfriend, Kumiko – the catalyst in Harding's artfully interwoven trilogy – Jonathan is forced to acknowledge the damage he has done. His photograph, while it carried no caption, projected the seated soldier as a guilty man, while Jim may in fact only have borne the burden of witnessing an atrocity. But seeing alone creates a kind of guilt, and nobody is more painfully aware of the witness's complicity than Jonathan, a photographer who has taken to hiding behind his camera, after years of concealing what he himself – as we gradually discover – once witnessed as a child.

Harding is a thoughtful and disciplined writer. Slowly, she allows us to appreciate the rift between runaway Jonathan and his older brother Richard, the sibling who stayed at home to run the Norfolk farm. Something that the family should have shared has been hidden. 'You saw,' Richard accuses Jonathan after their father Charlie's sudden death in a spinney (the small wood that plays the same recurring and symbolic role in the *Harvest* cycle as the derelict greenhouse in *The Go-Between*). Claire, the boys' mother, insists that Charlie Ashe's shocking end was an accident: against all evidence, she claims that a loaded gun must have accidentally discharged itself while its owner, a cautious man, clambered over a fence that Jonathan informs us – but chooses not to remind his mother – had never in reality existed.

Richard's growing anger with his obdurately reticent brother derives from his conviction that Jonathan had watched his father die, and then concealed that crucial fact of his own presence. Harding reveals a more complex truth. Jonathan, a child of 7, had indeed climbed out of bed in order to track his father across the farm's misty fields. He heard the shot, but all he ever saw was a recognizable shape on the ground, and the earth growing sodden as it blotted up spilt blood from a head that – horrifyingly – was no longer there. 'I didn't see anything happen,' Jonathan will always truthfully but mis-leadingly assert. Unable to destroy his mother's comforting act of self-deception, he adopts a camera as his new, protective eye, a kind of shield that distances him from personal involvement.

Cleverly, Harding keeps her readers in the dark about just how much Richard Ashe, a troubled boy who torments his brother for not sharing his knowledge, really did want to understand the truth about his adored father's bewildering death. Kumiko's perceptive questions about the complicity of a witness unsettle Jonathan more than Richard's clumsy aggression. So does his own bafflingly passive response to the unexpected suicide of a young girl at a Tokyo train station. He sees the approaching train, and then the crowd's sudden withdrawal, 'moved back like a wave by the men in white gloves'. Had he seen the girl close, he asks himself, would he have remained sufficiently detached to photograph her even as she jumped?

Harding presents Jonathan with a tougher moral challenge when she enables him to discover that Kumiko's grandfather, a gentle old man obsessively tending his bonsai (just as Claire Ashe wistfully tends her garden of French roses in England), was one of his father's adversaries in a war that would eventually cause a middle-aged farmer to blow out his brains in a Norfolk wood. A hint of future reconcil-iation between the troubled photographer and his haunted past surfaces in the final pages of *The Gun Room*, when Jonathan plans to send Kumiko a card, inviting her to visit the Ashes' English farm-house. The possible consequences of his suggestion hover unanswered throughout the novel's concluding pages.

Harding has always been interested in moral dilemmas and tests of conscience. *The Solitude of Thomas Cave* (2006) charts the troubled spirit of a seventeenth-century mariner whose response to grief and loss, as a test of his own fortitude, is to isolate himself for a year in the Arctic. *Painter of Silence* (2012) explores a silenced atrocity in Stalinist Romania through the unplanned reunion of two survivors — who had occupied very different social spheres — from within the same manorial household. These two novels stand alone, but we do Harding an injustice in treating her recent books — as most critics have — as if they, too, were independent works.

The Gun Room raises difficult questions. The second book in the trilogy, *Land of the Living* (2018), answers some of them by taking us back to Charlie Ashe's experiences in the jungles of Assam and still more remote Nagaland during the Second World War. There, unforgettably and terribly, Charlie came across a group of murdered Sikh soldiers whose eyes — while the captives still lived, bound to tree-trunks by the unfurled lengths of their own sacred turbans — had been gouged out by barbed wire. His own small team were massacred in a freak attack from which he himself was the sole fleet-footed survivor. Jonathan Ashe's guilt stems from having arrived too late to prevent his father's death. Charlie Ashe cannot forgive himself for having saved his own life by running away.

Other novelists have written about the horrors that took place during the fight to prevent Japan from invading India through Nagaland, a peace-loving province loyal to the British Crown. Harding adds a twist of her own by placing the guilt-ridden Charlie Ashe in the unexpectedly benevolent care of a community of Naga head-hunters; there, with disbelief, he penetrates the disguise of the young Japanese soldier, a deserter, who had murdered his comrades. As with the subsequent encounter in Tokyo between Jonathan, the witness, and Jim, the soldier he saw in Vietnam, the question of blame becomes inescapable: which of the two men, the disguised killer or the runaway, is the more culpable? Charlie, while hotly tempted to kill the terrified assassin, recognizes a disquieting connection that stays his hand.

Would the boy think he was a deserter too? . . . Now he thought about it, he wasn't sure himself. He [Charlie] thought of the others and how he came to be alone and he thought, well, yes, one might well think that was what he was . . . Perhaps it showed, the guilt in him.

Returning to England, Charlie marries Claire, from whom he successfully conceals the worst of his wartime experiences. Artfully, Harding juxtaposes Charlie's anguished memories with the tense tranquillity of a marriage upon which his unyielding silence about the past imposes a perpetual burden. 'She thought she could not bear all that was left unsaid,' Harding has Claire say in the closing pages, but as Charlie's wife, she knows that she has no option but to comply. 'She smiled and spoke lightly. That was her part, to be light.'

Harvest is the time of year at which Claire Ashe first discovers that she is pregnant. The title of the cycle's final book intimates that harvest is also the season in which hidden truths will finally be brought to the surface and revealed.

Women play a far more prominent role in *Harvest* (2021). Kumiko has already shown herself to be an astute poser of awkward questions. Arriving at the lonely Norfolk farm on a perfect summer day, she is too conscious of a buried past to be convinced by Claire's graceful attempt to present a rural idyll, a garden filled with the exquisite Malmaison roses with which she has banished the emptiness of her life. Gradually, as Claire warms to this bright, cheerfully dressed girl from Japan, a country she had always regarded as her husband's enemy, disquieting memories begin to emerge.

Skilfully, scene by scene, Harding builds up the sense of imminent disaster. Shifting time back to the years that followed Charlie Ashe's death, she allows Claire to witness her sons' ferocious response to the visit of a suitor for their widowed mother's hand. After he leaves the house, Claire finds the boys have broken into her cherished sanctuary, a greenhouse, where they have smashed an entire miniature city of seedling pots. They don't even bother to pause at her entrance.

How could they do this?

Another step, and she saw Richard's eyes dart to the glass above their heads. Would he have raised the hoe and smashed that too? With one final blow? The sky glittering down on them, glass breaking, falling, cutting boys' skin? Glass in their eyes. No, tears. Tears in all their eyes.

He's gone, she said. Now come in and have tea.

They left the ruins without a word.

Slowly, meticulously, Harding directs her cast of five towards a betrayal and a revelation which together provide both a shocking climax and a possible catharsis. Leaving England, Kamiko, the truth-teller, feels as though her words and actions have set the Ashe family's home on fire. In the book's final words: 'It suddenly seemed like arson what she had done.'

As with all of Harding's novels, the future remains unpredicted. What the *Harvest* cycle lays bare with a subtle mastery of language and structure – added to rare powers of observation that never falter – are the terrible, unforeseeable consequences of war. Harding's trilogy is a quiet masterpiece of understated tragedy.

MIRANDA SEYMOUR has most recently written a biography of another brilliant novelist, *I Used to Live Here Once: The Haunted Life of Jean Rhys* (2022).

Sounds of the City

MARK HUDSON

There are books that linger in the mind because of their stories, characters or settings. There are books of such tragic intensity you feel you'll take certain incidents and phrases with you to the grave. And there are books so funny that the mention of them induces an involuntary chuckle. Then there are the books that stay with you through the sheer verve and musicality of their language. *The Lonely Londoners* (1956) is that kind of book.

I first encountered Sam Selvon's masterpiece by chance when it was read on BBC Radio 4's *A Book at Bedtime* by the great Trinidadian-British actor Rudolph Walker. I was immediately entranced by the tragi-comic misadventures of Moses, Captain, Sir Galahad and the book's other fictional young West Indian immigrants, barely surviving in the bleak bedsits of post-war Notting Hill and Bayswater. But what captivated me most was the warmth, humour and gregarious energy of Selvon's writing, with its unmistakable undertow of pathos and melancholy. Embodied in the sway and lilt of Walker's voice, these were qualities I could sense resonating through the static of time, decades after the programme was broadcast.

The Lonely Londoners defines a pivotal moment in British social and cultural history: the arrival of what is now known as the Windrush Generation. The magnificent rhetorical roll of its language, couched in a subtly adapted Trinidadian dialect, makes it not just a vital snapshot of a place and time, but a universal masterpiece

Sam Selvon, *The Lonely Londoners* (1956)
Penguin · Pb · 160pp · £9.99 · ISBN 9780141188416

of the urban condition, a work that feels epic, though it is actually very short.

While I love the book's humour, it is its sense of the pathos of the immigrant experience, a feeling of permanent displacement and nostalgic yearning, that lingers in the memory. That is certainly the quality most evident in the opening passages, when 'on a grim winter's evening, when it had a kind of unrealness about London, with a fog sleeping restlessly over the city', the protagonist Moses Aloetta, an apparently grumpy but inwardly kind-hearted Trinidadian carpenter, gets himself out of his warm bed to head down to Waterloo 'to meet a fella who was coming from Trinidad on the boat train'.

This, you're instantly persuaded, is the Windrush moment as it mostly actually happened. Rather than the crowds of smartly dressed West Indians packed on to ocean liners, depicted in contemporary newsreels, we're shown a steady influx of shivering, bewildered individuals or small groups who are met by the watchful stares of compatriots they barely know. These are distant acquaintances of acquaintances who, if Moses is anything to go by, don't welcome new rivals in the struggle for lodging and employment, when they themselves are 'still catching their arse in Brit'n'.

Moses, who has been in Britain for a decade, worries that the latest wave of incomers are, as he observes, 'real hustlers, desperate'. Yet he feels obliged to help these 'boys' find work and places to stay, while making sure to scatter them around London: 'for you didn't want no concentrated areas in the Water [Bayswater, where he lives] – as it is, things bad enough already'.

Yet for all that Moses prides himself on his hard-headed realism, he finds himself beset by a sense of indefinable nostalgia and regret as he enters Waterloo Station, a sense of how little he's achieved in his time in London, and a yearning he never imagined he'd feel to be heading back towards the tropics.

The notion of 'blackness' is frequently invoked: in a memorable moment one of the characters, Sir Galahad, addresses the colour, berating it for all the problems he's facing. Yet ethnicity is only specified in relation to the few African characters. We're left to assume that the other 'boys' are Afro-Caribbean. In fact, while Selvon appears intensely involved in their thought processes and quasi-familial social relationships – and gives a sense of the half-humorous ambivalence between Trinidadians and Jamaicans – he himself was of Trinidadian-Indian heritage. Born in 1923, he worked as a journalist before moving to London in 1950, where he took various menial jobs including a clerical position at the Indian High Commission, while writing his first novel and articles for the *London Magazine* and the *New Statesman*. *The Lonely Londoners* began as a collection of anecdotes, but it didn't start to cohere until he shifted the literary frame from Standard English to what he called 'dialect'.

These anecdotes are framed as encounters with a cast of larger-than-life characters, as though we ourselves are moving through Moses's social networks in the cramped rooms and grimy pavements of Bayswater and Notting Hill – then both painfully run-down areas – where 'the boys' chase 'pieces of skin' (mostly white) and endlessly tap each other for funds.

Captain is a fly-by-night Nigerian law student, who has gone 'stupid when he arrive in the big city', abandoned his studies and had his allowance stopped by his father, a king no less. Dressed in a green-striped suit and a pair of suede shoes, Cap engages in a series of elaborate subterfuges designed to avoid his ever having to work and involving expensive possessions (other people's watches and mohair coats), rented rooms (again other people's), money (borrowed, but never repaid) and, of course, women. Of various European nationalities they all fall for his sweet and innocent smile. He even marries a French girl, who believes she's heading for a privileged life in Nigeria, but he absconds immediately, heading for the 'all night café in the Gate where Cap does always hang out, coasting lime over a cuppa or a cup of coffee, sitting there eyeing every woman and trying to make contact'.

At the other end of the spectrum is Sir Galahad, the incorrigible romantic, a 25-year-old Trinidadian who mysteriously doesn't feel the cold and arrives in midwinter London wearing a light tropical suit and carrying only a toothbrush. Like many of the characters he nurtures a mythic sense of the greatness of the metropolis, even as he struggles on its grimmer pavements. His ideal is to walk through the West End 'cool as a lord' and meet a 'craft' (a girl) at Piccadilly Circus, a place 'that represent life, that circus the beginning and ending of the world'.

Five Past Twelve, a weed-smoking van driver, so called because he's 'blacker than midnight', delights in provoking the socially aspirant Harris, a sometime Port of Spain street urchin who wants to assimilate at the higher levels of British society. The latter's attempt to stage a genteel steel band party in St Pancras Town Hall provides one of the book's comic highpoints.

With the observation that 'wherever in London that it have working class, there you will find a lot of spades' (a term used by the immigrants themselves), Selvon expands his view outward over the city with its contrasts between rich and poor and its divisions into self-contained worlds: 'it have people living in London who don't know what happening in the room next to them, far more the street, or how other people living'. Yet in this relatively innocent period before the 1958 Notting Hill riots there was still 'a kind of communal feeling with the working class and the spades, because when you poor things does level out'.

Observing the women who lost fiancés in the war and are now 'pottering about the Harrow Road like if they lost, a look in their eye as if the war happened unexpected and they still can't realize what happened to the old Brit'n', Selvon goes on a magnificent imaginative roll, his eye scanning the city, homing in on the window of a 'fully furnished flat (rent bout 10 or 15 guineas, Lord)', where a woman sleeps late 'after a night at the Savoy or Dorchester'. Hearing an old man in the street below singing 'in a high falsetto' she drops down a 'tanner' (six old pence). And whether she does that because the 'sound of that voice quavering in the cold outside touch the old heart' or as a mindless reflex makes no difference to the old man, Selvon observes.

Here we're given a more universal sense of a city in which everyone, whatever their ethnicity or economic status, seems fated to play a particular role, and where people give, whether to their friends or to the old fella playing the mouth organ beside the cinema queue, not out of generosity but from 'a kind of shame'.

With the arrival of summer Selvon's prose acquires a marvellous rhapsodic uplift in the book's climactic stream-of-consciousness. There's something positively Chaucerian, not just in the sense of nature's exuberant lustful profusion, but in the great, gulping phrases in which he evokes the girls promenading along Bayswater Road in their light summer frocks, the boys 'coasting lime' in the park with 'all them pretty pieces of skin taking suntan . . . and everywhere you turn the English people smiling isn't it a lovely day as if the sun burn away all the tightness and strain that was in their faces'. There isn't a comma, let alone a full stop, for almost ten ecstatic pages.

It's only when he mentions the negotiating of 'ten shillings or a pound' that it occurs to the reader that all these light-limbed young women thronging Hyde Park and Kensington Gardens are prostitutes of varying degrees of professionalism. You're left wondering if there was anyone in pre-permissive era London who wasn't somehow on the game.

The book ends on the same wistful note with which it began, as Moses stares into the Thames, wondering if all his experiences in London have taught him anything, and sensing beneath the boys' endless banter and storytelling 'a great aimlessness, a great restless swaying movement that leaving you standing in the same spot'. Yet he senses beneath these feelings 'a greatness and a vastness . . . and though he ain't getting no happiness out of the cogitations he still pondering'.

While you may start *The Lonely Londoners* with the impression that you're experiencing immigrant life told straight from the hip, you may conclude, as I did, that it is as much a work of observation and imagination as it is of personal experience. Selvon imbues his novel with the rhythms of the Caribbean marketplace, calypso and the church sermon. And taking wild liberties with literary form, darting in and out of Standard English with literary quotes and cultural references, he demonstrates the endless expansiveness and elasticity of those rhythms. That's what makes this book not just a marvellously vivid record of a time and a place, but also a great work of modernist literature. *The Lonely Londoners* is both a snapshot of the painful birth pangs of multi-cultural Britain, and a formative element in the creation of that world. I wish it had been five times as long.

MARK HUDSON's novel *The Music in My Head*, about a white British music entrepreneur stranded in a fictional African city, was praised by the *Village Voice* as offering 'music from the inside and a mad sprawl of a book that evokes it every which way'. His other books include *Our Grandmothers' Drums*, *Coming Back Brockens* and *Titian, the Last Days*. He is also the art critic of the *Independent*.

Political Life

DAISY HAY

In *Slightly Foxed* no. 73 I wrote about the solace I found, during the first year of the pandemic, in listening to Timothy West's brilliant recordings of Anthony Trollope's Barchester novels. I couldn't bear to stop listening when I reached the end of *The Last Chronicle of Barset*, so I followed Plantagenet Palliser and the Duke of Omnium out of Barsetshire and into the books in which they take up starring roles. Originally labelled collectively as Trollope's 'parliamentary novels', today this series is more commonly known as 'the Palliser novels' after the family whose domestic and political fortunes form its connecting thread.

The shape of the Palliser series is slightly unwieldy. Trollope wrote of it as a quartet with two subsidiary titles, although he found it hard to believe that anyone would treat it as he intended. 'Who will read *Can You Forgive Her?*, *Phineas Finn*, *Phineas Redux* and *The Prime Minister* consecutively, in order that they may understand the characters of the Duke of Omnium, of Plantagenet Palliser, and of Lady Glencora?' he wondered in his *Autobiography*. 'Who will ever know that they should so be read?' Two further novels – *The Eustace Diamonds* and *The Duke's Children* –

Anthony Trollope's six Palliser novels (*Can You Forgive Her?*, *Phineas Finn*, *Phineas Redux*, *The Prime Minister*, *The Eustace Diamonds* and *The Duke's Children*), read by Timothy West, are all available to download from Audible Books: visit www.audible.co.uk.

interweave themselves among this quartet chronologically. I organized my listening in accordance with Trollope's scheme, skipping straight from *Phineas Finn* to *Phineas Redux*, and returning to *The Eustace Diamonds* and *The Duke's Children* after I reached the end of *The Prime Minister*.

The Palliser novels, published between 1864 and 1880, do not drop you in a specific place as do the Barsetshire chronicles. They immerse you instead in a particular moment in British history when, in the 1860s and 1870s, Liberal and Conservative parliamentary factions fought internecine battles over the structures of power in both Britain and Ireland. These are novels that cohere thematically rather than geographically, but, like Trollope's earlier series, they also offer the reader – or, in my case, the listener – the pleasure of following the same characters in and out of other people's stories, until they become as familiar as friends.

The Palliser series opens with *Can You Forgive Her?*, first published in serial form between 1864 and 1865. Its central character is Alice Vavasor, whose vacillation between two suitors – her bounder cousin George and steady, dull John Grey – forms the crux of the story, and the topic of the title's question. Trollope himself was proud of the novel, although he claimed that its heroine was not an attractive character. (*Punch* agreed, renaming the novel *Can You Stand Her?*) Alice's quandary gives rise to a question that recurs throughout the Palliser series, namely 'What should a woman do with her life?' In *Can You Forgive Her?* Alice finds one answer to this question when, after much heartache, she chooses security over excitement in the person of John Grey. Ultimately John Grey leaves her 'no alternative but to be happy', but happiness comes for Alice at the cost of the independence of mind and spirit that rendered her so unlikeable in the eyes of both her creator and some of Trollope's more censorious original readers.

The romantic travails of her wealthy aunt, Mrs Greenow, form a second narrative strand, but there is one crucial difference: Mrs

Greenow has money, and she therefore has the ability to make both her suitors dance to her tune. Lady Glencora also has money – lots of it – but in her case a great fortune has been the means of trapping her, as she is forced into a dynastic union with Plantagenet Palliser by scheming relatives from both families. Like Alice, Lady Glencora has given her love to a cad and a bounder, and at the centre of *Can You Forgive Her?* is her torment as she attempts to decide whether to stay in a comfortable, loveless marriage or whether to elope and break her husband's heart.

If Alice Vavasor's story has a happy ending, the opposite is true of Lady Glencora's. She stays in her marriage and makes the best of it, touched by her husband's devotion and his willingness to sacrifice a political career in order to keep her. She finds an answer to the question 'What should a woman do with her life?' in building an existence that is full of friends and interests, becoming a political hostess whose success eventually rivals that achieved by her Prime Minister husband.

Trollope himself recognized that one of the triumphs of the series is that, although their circumstances change, the Pallisers themselves remain recognizable throughout.

> It was my study that these people, as they grew in years, should encounter the changes which come upon us all; and I think I have succeeded. The Duchess of Omnium, when she is playing the part of Prime Minister's wife, is the same woman as that Lady Glencora who almost longs to go off with Burgo Fitzgerald, but yet knows that she will never do so; and the Prime Minister Duke, with his wounded pride and sore spirit, is he who, for his wife's sake, left power and place when they were first offered to him; – but they have undergone the changes which a life so stirring as theirs would naturally produce.

For the reader who follows these characters through the novels the reward is immense, and the complexities of Lady Glencora's compromised but nevertheless rich happiness in later life are far more interesting than Alice Vavasor's tidy happy ending.

One of the motifs running through all the Palliser novels is that young women are much better off avoiding dashing, mysterious men. Emily Wharton, one of the sub-heroines of *The Prime Minister*, marries her cad with disastrous effects, and is only saved from her mistake when the cad destroys himself courtesy of the trains at Clapham Junction. Women don't always do better, though, if they settle for the safe bet. In *Phineas Finn* Lady Laura Standish marries dour, rich Robert Kennedy of her own volition but is then trapped in a nightmare as the extent of Kennedy's mad Presbyterianism becomes apparent.

It was while I was listening to *Phineas Finn*, and subsequently to *Phineas Redux*, that the Palliser novels took an iron hold on my attention. The hero of these paired titles is an Irishman of modest means who attempts to make his way in the world of British politics. Like the women whose uncertain futures Trollope depicts so thoughtfully, Phineas is entirely dependent on others for political and personal success, because he is both poor and an outsider. He retires from London life buffeted by his experiences at the end of *Phineas Finn* but returns in the sequel to fight for his political career and, after some dramatic plot twists, for his liberty and his life. *Phineas Redux* unfolds the slow tragedy of Lady Laura's loveless marriage, but it counterbalances this with the evolving relationship between Phineas and Madame Max Goesler, the beautiful, wealthy widow of a Jewish financier whose bravery saves both Phineas's neck and the house of the Duke of Omnium.

Phineas Redux is a truly wonderful novel, indeed the standout discovery of my hours with the Pallisers. It has plenty of drama to keep you turning the pages, or in my case pressing play on the audiobook, but it is also a fascinating portrait of a world in which fake news, malicious reporting, gossip and rumour can break reputations over the course of a single day. In the unlikely alliance of Lady

Glencora and Madame Max it has one of Trollope's most brilliant representations of female friendship, and it nimbly combines politics with romance. Trollope was always mindful of the need to balance political set-pieces with domestic drama: 'If I write politics for my own sake, I must put in love and intrigue, social incidents, with perhaps a dash of sport, for the benefit of my readers.' His view was that he had succeeded in making this balance work in the *Phineas* novels, although he later wrote that it had been a mistake to make his hero Irish, earning him only 'an added difficulty in obtaining sympathy and affection for a politician belonging to a nationality whose politics are not respected in England'.

Phineas gets his happy ending when he marries Madame Max Goesler, and when another cad – the *soi disant* Reverend Mr Emilius – is proved by the exertions of Madame Max to have committed the murder for which Phineas himself has been imprisoned. Mr Emilius's story is told at greater length in the first of the two titles that sit between the parliamentary stories to complete the Palliser series. His novel is *The Eustace Diamonds*, a police-detective caper in which pretty, shallow Lizzie Eustace outwits the outraged society matrons who comment, like a Greek chorus, on her determination to retain possession of a valuable necklace that she maintains (untruthfully) has been left to her under the terms of the late Sir Eustace's will. By the time of the final parliamentary novel, *The Prime Minister*, however, Lady Eustace has been reduced to a life lived on the fringes of London society, alongside the cads and the bounders of whom she is a female equivalent.

The Trollope cad, whether male or female, moves through the world of the Palliser series untroubled by morality, motivated only by personal gain. At various points it appears as if the cad is on the ascendant, threatening the status quo as preserved by the Pallisers and their friends. In the end, though, it is a version of pragmatic continuity that triumphs.

In the final novel of the series, *The Duke's Children*, Lady Glencora has died and Plantagenet Palliser, now the Duke of Omnium himself, is left alone to confront a world in which his children appear to hold very different values to his. His heir, Lord Silverbridge, wishes to marry an American heiress; his younger son loses money at cards and gets himself expelled from Cambridge following an illicit trip to the Derby. His daughter, meanwhile, will not accept for herself the sacrifice forced upon her mother, and eventually the Duke is persuaded to let her have her way and marry the man she loves. Ultimately it is another outsider, Madame Max (now happily married to Phineas Finn), who helps him to see that his family's name need not be upheld only at the cost of his children's happiness. So as the series closes the Pallisers themselves have 'no alternative but to be happy', but they find their happiness when they are collectively willing to compromise in accordance with the reality of the changing times in which they live.

Now that some time has passed since I listened to the Palliser novels, however, I realize it's not the happy endings that have stayed with me. Instead it's the stories of the women – Alice Vavasor, Lady Glencora, Madame Max, Mrs Greenow, Lady Eustace, Emily Wharton, Lady Laura Kennedy and many others – that remain in my mind. All of them are constrained to answer the question posed in *Can You Forgive Her?* What is a woman to do with her life? For none is the answer to that question straightforward. Yet these characters are never merely vehicles through which an argument about the position of women is mounted. Trollope lived with and through his characters, and to him their lives mattered because of who they were, and not just because of what they represented. That is why they make such ideal companions for listening, because they live alongside the reader in the imagination of their creator. 'They have been as real to me as free trade was to Mr Cobden, or the dominion of a party to Mr Disraeli,' Trollope wrote, as he considered the series. 'As I have not been able to speak from the benches of the House of Commons, or to thunder from platforms, or to be efficacious as a lecturer, they have served me as safety-valves by which to deliver my soul.'

DAISY HAY is the author of *Dinner with Joseph Johnson: Books and Friendship in a Revolutionary Age*. When not moonlighting as *Slightly Foxed*'s occasional Trollope correspondent she teaches English Literature and Life Writing at the University of Exeter. You can also hear her in Episode 43 of our podcast, discussing literary salons and the early days of publishing in London.

The illustrations in this article are by Gwen Raverat from *The Bedside Barsetshire* (1949).

The Man Who . . .

MARTIN EDWARDS

The only fan letter I ever wrote was to Julian Symons (1912–94). A polymath – poet, editor, biographer, historian, novelist and reviewer – his non-fiction books encompassed Dickens, Carlyle, Wyndham Lewis, the General Strike and the Gordon Relief Expedition, but what fascinated me were his crime novels and his critical insights into the genre.

His *The Progress of a Crime* (1960) was the first contemporary crime novel I read, and it was quite unlike the traditional puzzles of Agatha Christie and Arthur Conan Doyle that I'd devoured as a boy. The storyline, based on a real-life miscarriage of justice involving a killing on Clapham Common, was much bleaker, and his use of irony and the crisp way in which he wrote – Symons never wasted words – drew me in. I began to seek out more.

One in particular I found especially gripping. *The Man Who Killed Himself* (1967) represented a dazzling departure from his earlier work. Symons had concocted whodunits in the classic tradition as well as novels of psychological suspense and a Cold War thriller, *The Broken Penny* (1953), with a protagonist based on his friend George Orwell. He'd also won 'best novel of the year' awards in both Britain and the United States – and not for the same book. But like most writers of distinction, he wasn't content to rest on his laurels.

Julian Symons's crime novels *The Colour of Murder* (1957), *The Progress of a Crime* (1960) and *The Belting Inheritance* (1965) are available in paperback as British Library Crime Classics. His other books mentioned in this article are out of print, but we can obtain second-hand copies.

Although a few characters make more than one appearance in his novels, he never created a memorable series detective. Partly as a result, his books were never bestsellers; he acknowledged that his 'abomination' of series sleuths was 'commercially foolish' but added that: '[Raymond] Chandler once said that the puzzle plot is a kind of crutch needed by the crime writer, and much the same is true of the series detective. A crutch is useful, no doubt, but it is better to stand on two legs.' The argument is flawed, because the best crime writers are capable of developing their characters over the course of a number of books, but although Symons's determination to keep trying something different led to inconsistency, his literary ambition meant that even his weaker books have merit.

He was in his mid-fifties when he decided on a fresh approach to his fiction. This produced *The Man Who Killed Himself*, a novel often grouped with the two that followed, *The Man Whose Dreams Came True* (1968) and *The Man Who Lost His Wife* (1970). Although the characters and storylines in each are very different, the 'Man Who' stories reflect broadly similar preoccupations. Years later, he explained the thinking behind his shift of focus:

A novelist's strategies, the approaches he makes to his material, change with the years; even the material changes, or seems to him to do so, those raw shapes of life he is trying to coerce into a pattern . . . There is a moment when one realizes that the old kind of plotting won't do, that the order which had seemed to serve well over a number of books no longer satisfies.

So, halfway down the Sixties, I realized . . . that I wanted to write something more loosely constructed, giving scope for a more casual interweaving of characters and perhaps for increased depth in considering them. I had done with novels about the police and the administration of justice . . . [The 'Man Who' novels] are the result, books in which there is no puzzle to be solved, but an attempt to show the social ironies of urban life . . .

and people, seen realistically although with a touch of exaggeration.

He set the tone of *The Man Who Killed Himself* in the opening lines:

> In the end Arthur Brownjohn killed himself, but in the beginning he made up his mind to murder his wife. He did so on the day that Major Easonby Mellon met Patricia Parker. Others might have come to such a decision earlier but Arthur Brownjohn was a patient and, as all those who knew him agreed, a timid and long-suffering man. When people say that a man is long-suffering, they mean that they see no reason why he should not suffer for ever.

Arthur is an unsuccessful inventor, married to a wealthy bully called Clare who has the good sense not to invest in his eccentric business ventures. His penchant for fantasy and escapism finds an outlet when he begins to lead a double life. Suppressed aspects of his personality come to the fore when he creates the extrovert Major Easonby Mellon, who runs a highly dubious matrimonial bureau. In the guise of Mellon, he is married to pleasant but naïve Joan, and so as to explain his frequent absences from their home in Clapham, he has managed to persuade her that he is actually a secret agent. (These passages enable Symons to satirize the James Bond phenomenon, with entertaining results.) And then Joan shocks Arthur by telling him that a man called Flexner – a fellow spy who is the product of Arthur's imagination – has called at the house while he was out. What on earth is going on?

The plot thickens and darkens as Arthur becomes infatuated with an attractive client of the matrimonial bureau and forges a cheque in Clare's name to fund a new invention. His fascination with the famous old murder cases recounted in *Notable British Trials* leads him to dream about Clare's demise, and before long he comes up with a cunning plan to get away with murder. Twists of fate abound, but ultimately this story is a study of psychological disintegration. Symons had tackled that subject before, notably in *The Thirty-First of February* (1950), and he would revisit it subsequently, but this novel stands out for its sheer zest and wit. On first reading, I loved it.

When I revisited *The Man Who Killed Himself* decades later, I detected the influence of two writers, very different from each other, whom Symons knew and admired. There is more than a touch of Patricia Highsmith about his exploration of the character flaws that lead a seemingly ordinary individual into criminality. His portrayal of Arthur also owes something to that of Dr Bickleigh in Francis Iles's masterly suspense novel of 1930, *Malice Aforethought*. But Symons fashioned these elements into a distinctive entertainment which captured the anything-goes mood of the Swinging Sixties.

The novel was swiftly adapted into a film starring Donald Pleasence, Shelley Winters and Terry-Thomas, with several British acting stalwarts among the supporting cast, but it was never released in UK cinemas. What went wrong? Well, there's a clue in the excruciating title: *Arthur? Arthur!* The story is presented as a black comedy, with the subtler elements stripped out and a completely different resolution. Pleasence performs the dual roles of Arthur Brownjohn and Easonby Mellon with gusto and there are some funny moments, but overall it is a mess. For the curious, the film is now viewable online, courtesy of BFI Player.

The Man Whose Dreams Came True was another engaging study of a fantasist who becomes embroiled in murder, while *The Man Who Lost His Wife* was a less successful attempt to emulate Highsmith. 'The Man Who' books may not really form a trilogy, but they explore character and crime with irony and teasing wit. As Symons said, they are 'all emphatically books about town life and people, seen realistically although with a touch of exaggeration . . . With the three books completed, I appear to have worked out the vein and have never returned to it.'

He continued to experiment, venturing into historical mysteries and Sherlockiana, even introducing himself as a character in the unorthodox mystery *Death's Darkest Face* (1990). His most celebrated book was *Bloody Murder* (1972), an elegantly written history of the genre which charted its progress (as he saw it) 'from detective story to crime novel'. Unquestionably his report of the death of the classic detective story was exaggerated. Not long after *Bloody Murder* first appeared, Colin Dexter introduced Inspector Morse, disrupting the smooth course of literary evolution that Symons had described. Today the truth is clear: traditional detective fiction hadn't disappeared, nor had the public appetite for it faded. Books of that kind had simply fallen out of critical fashion.

Bloody Murder isn't perfect, but it expanded my knowledge and understanding of the genre and I've returned to it a hundred times. As a young graduate, trying to write my first crime novel, I wrote to Symons to express my enthusiasm for *The Man Who Killed Himself* and *Bloody Murder*. To my delight, he replied generously and thoughtfully, and many years later I enjoyed meeting him at crime writers' conferences. Today, though, despite the fact that he was the most garlanded male British crime novelist of his generation, most of his books are out of print. I've been glad to reintroduce three of his early novels to a new readership in the twenty-first century through the British Library's Crime Classics series and I keep hoping that *The Man Who Killed Himself* will be brought back into print. Meanwhile I remember him fondly as the man who introduced me to the rich possibilities of contemporary crime fiction.

MARTIN EDWARDS is the author of twenty-one crime novels and a newly published history of mystery, *The Life of Crime*. You can also hear him in Episode 33 of our podcast, discussing the Golden Age of crime writing.

Trouble at the Vatican

SUZI FEAY

'How very Corvine of you,' I purred to the witty author who had just made a remark as savage as it was exquisitely expressed. His eyes widened in surprise, then took on a gleam of approval. In an instant we recognized each other as fans of that most recondite of authors and enigmatic of literary personalities: Fr. Rolfe, also known as Baron Corvo.

As a gay writer, Rolfe has gained a small but devoted readership denied to him in life. The sly ambiguity of that 'Fr.' – it stands for Frederick but could be read as 'Father' – is typical of this slippery individual, who liked to pose as a man of the cloth. After being rejected for the priesthood, a perceived injustice Rolfe raged at for the rest of his life, he took up his mysterious title of Baron, conferred, he claimed, by an elderly member of a noble clan whom he had befriended in Italy. Another of his incarnations was 'F. Austin', and for a time he wrote a furious series of letters under the name of Frank W. Hochheimer.

Of all the works he wrote in his short life, *Hadrian the Seventh* (1904) is the best known. It was acclaimed by D. H. Lawrence ('first-rate') and later by Graham Greene, who was no doubt attracted by its intense atmosphere of heavy-breathing Catholicism. *Hadrian* is currently available as a Penguin Classic, albeit with a few typos that would have dismayed its fastidious author. On first glance it's a novel about an impoverished middle-aged Englishman, George Arthur

Fr. [Frederick] Rolfe [Baron Corvo], *Hadrian the Seventh* (1904)
Penguin · Pb · 368pp · £9.99 · ISBN 9780241313022

Rose, who unexpectedly – even miraculously – becomes Pope, only to fall prey to calumniators from his past. Yet such are the weird billows and currents of emotion that pulse beneath the prose, such are the eccentricities of its central character and the specifics of his grudges and obsessions, it's impossible not to suspect that this is more than pure fiction.

On reading the novel in 1925, twelve years after the death of its unhappy author, the young bibliophile A. J. A. Symons was inspired to embark on *The Quest for Corvo* (see *SF* no. 46), as his subsequent 'experiment in biography' was titled. It was a timely investigation, as many of the men Rolfe had crossed swords with were still around. Symons had a lot of untangling to do to get at the truth behind the alternative identities and myths Rolfe spun around himself.

Born in London's Cheapside in 1860 as Frederick William Rolfe, he converted to Catholicism in his mid-twenties, and the faith was to prove his succour and his bane (mostly his bane) for the rest of his life. It's not surprising that his superiors deemed him unsuitable for the priesthood, considering his prickly nature and tendency to paranoia. Having some artistic talent, Rolfe decided to make his way as an artist, journalist and novelist, but he never forgave those who had thwarted him.

Today, there is no doubt he would be an Internet troll of the most persistent

Frederick Rolfe's self-portrait, 1903

and vituperative kind. Bursts of kindness and a magnetic personality drew admirers, but Rolfe proved incapable of retaining friendships, alienating anyone who tried to help him by subjecting them to torrents of outrageous demands, abuse and accusations. How his victims must have shuddered on receiving an envelope addressed in Rolfe's exquisite hand, knowing that what lay within would be another vicious diatribe. Thinly disguised former collaborators, priests and would-be patrons turn up in the pages of *Hadrian the Seventh*, savagely upbraided for their perfidy towards the blameless protagonist.

Canon Carmont, a fellow trainee priest during Rolfe's ill-fated stint at the Scots College in Rome, sardonically observed to Symons that his former friend 'was good enough to make me a Cardinal' in its pages.

Eccentric, pedantic and weirdly coloured by revenge though it is, *Hadrian* is a ripping read, once you accustom yourself to the Corvine style, described by the *Oxford Companion to English Literature* as 'highly ornate and idiosyncratic; his vocabulary is arcane, his allusions erudite'. This after all is a man who subtitled his novella *Don Tarquinio* 'A Kataleptic Phantasmatic Romance'. Rolfe has no truck with anything so commonplace as a prologue; preceding Chapter One is a 'Prooimion'. In a mere handful of pages the reader may encounter such oddities as 'picric', 'lethific', 'epiphytic' or 'saxificous'. Adding to the mystic muddle, Rolfe's spelling is strange; Cystine instead of Sistine, for example. The Vatican generally appears without its definite article. It's the work of a stubborn autodidact and wilful pedant. But there is much to enjoy.

In the opening pages, George Arthur Rose is a vivid presence in his tiny attic bedroom-studio, musing on his impecunious fate, upbraiding himself for his own weakness and failure, and amused by the antics of his little cat, Flavio. George, with his endless cheap roll-ups, indifference to food, penchant for working out with dumb-bells and morbid fear of lizards, bears a distinct resemblance to the author.

Perhaps we all harbour a secret desire to return to the scene of our greatest ignominy in triumph, ready to punish or pardon adversaries and nay-sayers. If so, Rolfe raised a common fantasy to high art. In that 'Prooimion', George is visited in his humble lodgings by a repentant bishop and cardinal seeking to entice him back to the priesthood. The account of his life that George Rose gives them is a mirror of his creator's. After being trounced by George's superior intelligence, the cardinal announces he is there to offer 'Amends and restitution . . . you are simply to say in what form you will accept this act of justice from us.' George receives this handsome tribute with more grace than his creator was ever to muster.

The scene shifts to Rome, where argumentative cardinals in conclave are deadlocked over the election of a new pope. George, newly frocked, is gazing all about him when there's a sudden commotion and an astonishing summons. 'The Sacred College has elected thee to be the successor of St Peter. Wilt thou accept the pontificality?' George becomes Hadrian, named after the only other English pope. The transformation is sudden and profound; his pronouns promptly become capitalized. Before turning His attention to the overhaul of the Catholic Church and, beyond that, nothing less than the whole world order, His first job is to oversee the redecoration of the pontifical apartments in a sober, restrained, yet high-spec fashion.

We can take a moment here to appreciate how fulfilling this exuberant fantasy must have been to its impoverished author. The zest and energy of the story, its dizzying sensuous detail, form a tragic counterpoint to Rolfe's actual situation. The novel is written in such a bravura style that even the more shameless moments of self-congratulation raise a wry smile rather than outright derision. Sceptical cardinals are soon won over, astounded by the new Pontiff's grasp of world affairs; emperors and kings bow down before him. Hadrian begins drafting a series of Letters to the nations of the world, all received with awe and rapture. He redraws the world map, creating powerful new blocs and erasing France and Russia in the process, while England becomes 'the Ninefold Kingdom'. He sells off Vatican treasures and helps Himself to the papal bank account – all for good causes. Some of His acts are highly prescient. By making Joan of Arc a saint, for example, Rolfe anticipates the Papacy by almost two decades.

Hadrian's analysis of the world order at the turn of the century is as eccentric as everything else in the novel but has a quirky charm. For readers of *The Quest for Corvo* there's an especial piquancy in the lofty exchange between Hadrian and the German Kaiser, in which they ponder the annexation of Austria, the threat from Russia and the fate of the Balkans. One of Symons's informants reported that Rolfe occasionally referred to his godfather, 'slightly emphasizing the word'. Then one day, when they were discussing a newspaper article about the Kaiser, Rolfe suddenly observed: 'So my godfather's been at it again, has he?'

Hadrian is perforce celibate, but there is scope for a chaste passion with the young prelates in whom the Pope takes a slightly more than paternal interest. The solitary female character to appear in the strictly masculine world of *Hadrian* is treated with impatient contempt. Mrs Crowe has come to Rome to reignite her unrequited passion for the former George Rose. She's accompanied by a resentful political activist, Jerry Sant of the 'LibLab' party, thoroughly opposed to Hadrian's spiritual authority. Rolfe, a natural aristocrat of spirit, if not blood, mocks Sant's left-wing attitudes with lofty sarcasm in the book's most amusing pages, but Hadrian underestimates the malice of the pair at His peril.

Like its author, *Hadrian the Seventh* is strange, passionate, idiosyncratic, unconsciously silly and decidedly flawed, but the book wouldn't be improved by removal of those flaws; rather it would lose its essential flavour. In sticking so stubbornly to his self-willed, self-exculpating fantasy Fr. Rolfe created something unique, and there will always be readers eager to follow the swish of his cassock down the sumptuous, susurrating halls of his imagination.

SUZI FEAY is currently President of the Critics Circle and writes regularly for *The Spectator*, *The Tablet* and the *Financial Times*.

Oh Sir John!

PATRICK WELLAND

In 1976, a year remembered in the UK for its blazing summer, publication of a scabrous novel so inflamed a group of academics that they burned copies in the library at Reading University. Less delicate souls embraced the book. It won that year's Hawthornden Prize for Literature and the Guardian Fiction Prize, garnering encomiums from reviewers who struggled to match its exuberant prose. The *New York Times* called it a 'fresco of groinwork'; *Time Magazine* welcomed a 'swollen, rumbustical bladder of a book . . . unstoppable as a rush of sack to the kidneys'; Anthony Burgess praised its 'wordy divagations of a more monkish (Rabelaisian) tradition' and included it among his 99 best modern novels.

The book is a curiosity: the 'autobiography' of a fictionalized dramatic character loosely based on a historical figure. In increasingly puritanical times it may still be found offensive, but this would be to miss the point. Lack of restraint is fundamental to what is, in effect, a 450-page ironic joke, written in the knowledge (and, no doubt, hope) that it would scandalize as much as please. I first read the book forty years ago and I still love it for its boisterous anarchy.

So, who is it that disgusts and delights? He is that 'trunk of humours, that bolting-hutch of beastliness, that huge bombard of sack . . . that grey Iniquity, that father Ruffian, that vanity in years'. It is Falstaff – 'Jack to my familiars' – brought to rambunctious life by Robert Nye.

Robert Nye, *Falstaff* (1976), is out of print but we can obtain second-hand copies.

Variously a reporter, milkman, postman and jobbing gardener, Nye was born in London in 1939 to a civil servant and a Welsh farmer's daughter whose 'innate peasant story-telling ability' imbued in him a love of the oral tradition. He was foremost a poet and, for twenty-five years, poetry critic for *The Times*. But after writing stories for his three young sons, he turned to fiction as a sideline to indulge his fascination with mythology, legend and history. Over a period of thirty years, he produced nine novels on figures from Merlin and Faust to Byron and Joan of Arc's Marshal, Gilles de Rais. 'My stories', he said, 'have their sources in dreams which more than one person has dreamt, in ballads, jests and yarns, and in those folk tales which are, as it were, the dreams of the people coming to us without the interference of our own identity.'

Falstaff was Nye's second novel, taking the form of a 100-chapter memoir dictated over 100 days to six secretaries as the braggart knight nears death at his home in Caister Castle, Norfolk, in 1459. Grandiosely entitled the *Acta Domini Johannis Fastolfe* or *Life and Valliant Deeds of Sir John Faustoff* or *The Hundred Days War, as told by Sir John Fastolf, KG*, at face value it is a magnificent riot of bawdy, constructing a life of sufficiently disgraceful excess to befit its swaggering protagonist. Yet it is not all boozing, brawling and bedding. Alert readers will enjoy a stream of sly jokes and camouflaged allusions as well as obscure references to religion, folklore and historical events which may or may not have occurred. Anachronistic nods to authors, philosophers and poets (among them Keats, Joyce, Descartes and Pope) are so seamlessly inserted they can pass unnoticed. Quotes from *Henry IV Parts 1* and *2* and *The Merry Wives of Windsor* dot the text which, as it is supposedly written 150 years before the Henriad, cheekily implies that Shakespeare plagiarized Falstaff's words.

Intoxicated by his own importance, Falstaff is incapable of sticking to his script and peppers his recollections with bizarre digressions under chapter headings such as 'About Swinge-Bucklers and Bona-Robas', 'About Leprechauns and St Boniface', 'About St John Fastolf's

Prick', 'About Honour and Onions' and so forth. Occasionally, he breaks from the narrative to mesh limbs with his willing teenage niece Miranda, down stupefying quantities of sack or verbally abuse his secretaries who dutifully record their humiliation. He is fond of lists: of the different spellings of his name (66), of Miranda's nicknames for his 14-inch 'mainspring' (23), of Popes (34), giants (51) and victuals consumed at a sitting (17 game birds, 22 wines and 4 yards of black pudding). At the end, a three-page inventory of the contents of Caister Castle is followed by a nine-page Last Will and Testament. It also contains crudely drawn illustrations, six showing the different sonic natures of a fart. It is highly eccentric.

One secretary, Falstaff's sceptical stepson Scrope, asks if what he is recording is true and receives the magisterial reply: 'My belly gives me licence to give imaginative body to what is essentially sparse, even skeletal material: memories, biographies, jokes, histories, letters, images, fragments. I make patterns of my fragments. This book is the pattern I am making.' He tells us 'truth is not a goddess or any other manner of immutable or immortal'. We are warned.

Vainglorious from the outset, Falstaff claims in the opening sentence that he was conceived under a fig tree growing on the ten-yard erection of the Giant of Cerne Abbas carved on a hillside in Dorset. At 12, he becomes page to the Duke of Norfolk. Addressing the reader as 'Sir' or 'Madam', as if in conversation, he says he spent the next three years dressed as a girl for the pleasure of the Duchess and her maids Portia, Rosalind and Celia (Falstaff's stepsister is Ophelia, his pet rat Desdemona and his cook, Macbeth), before going to war as squire to the Duke. This is the cue for some preposterously inflated assertions such as triumphing at the Siege of Kildare by pelting Irish besiegers with hogskins of poteen and dispatching French sailors at the Battle of Sluys by breaking their skulls with hogsheads of sack. Scrope suspects his stepfather of inventing whimsy about this battle, for the engagement inconveniently took place in 1340, forty years before Falstaff was born.

In contrast to the absurdity of such braggadocio, Nye paints a picture of medieval Merrie England that is wholly credible in its earthy vigour and sheer weirdness. Here is Falstaff arriving in London as a young man, wearing shoes 'so long and pointed that they needed jewelled chains to hold their toes fastened curled up to my knees'. His codpiece open, and tied at the top with a bunch of ribbons, he walks with minstrels, merchants, mendicants and monks; strolling musicians play rottes, gitterns, citoles and mandores; jokers walk on stilts and jugglers on their hands; London Bridge is piled with tumbledown four-storey houses spanning a noisome tunnel in which a space is kept clear for jousting. Occasionally, Nye's poesy, which infuses so much of the writing, breaks cover. 'The rivers flashed. The trees were leaved with light. Windmills wove the wind.'

Nye has tremendous fun tweaking familiar scenes from the Henriad, such as the robbery at Gadshill (Jack proposes three versions of the 'truth'), carousing at the Boar's Head (filthy behaviour with Doll Tearsheet) and scrapes with Nym, Bardolph and Pistol (the latter two allowed their own unlikely stories). How did Hotspur really die on the battlefield of Shrewsbury? And what three ill-advised words from Falstaff were the cause of Hal's later repudiation of his old companion in riot? A mix of pathos and defiance creeps in as the fat knight recalls his 'mad lad, sweet lag, rascalliest prince'. He protests: 'In me, by me, *through* me, he was prepared for the throne of England and France. The Battle of Agincourt was won on the playing fields of Gadshill.' The use of Wellington's quote about the Battle of Waterloo is typical: one of the joys of the book is spotting Nye's plunder of familiar literary phrases.

It is a tribute to Nye's fertile imagination that he devotes only a quarter of the novel to the period of Falstaff's life with which we are familiar. For this is a book as expansive as Falstaff's belly and as colourful, ribald and uncontrolled as the medieval world it describes.

Elsewhere, we are given vivid descriptions of the plague and the battle-field horrors of Agincourt and Shrewsbury. We read of the death of Henry IV (the 'Leper King'), the coronation and death of Henry V ('Harry the Prig'), of May Day, Pope Joan, Bartholomew Fair, of the sieges of Rouen and Harfleur and of the ludicrous Battle of Herrings at Rouvray. Throughout these dubious engagements, Falstaff is ever more Flashman than swordsman. The real Sir John Fastolf, on whom our hero is said to be based, fled the 1429 Battle of Patay through cowardice. Falstaff turns his back on the fighting because, he says, he saw a white roe deer with the face of Joan of Arc. It is a touch of magical realism that encapsulates the strangeness of a world in which superstition still rubbed shoulders with religion, and mystery was allowed its part in life.

As the book draws to a close, the unrepentant old goat is losing his sight and cannot read what is being taken down by his amanuenses. Unknown to him, Scrope, outraged at being ordered to record such a litany of disgrace, inserts his own contributions, undermining the entire history. The narrative, he says, is a 'hellish pack of lies' written by a devil: 'He writes a kind of requiem for a life he never lived. I, Scrope, tell you the truth about him and about his book. *This is a work of fiction.*' Is it so? The last word goes to Falstaff in a death-bed confession.

Nye, who died in 2016, was quietly satisfied with *Falstaff*, saying, 'In writing it I found myself, my own voice and pitch.' This is a gar-gantuan banquet of a book worthy of Shakespeare's 'stuffed cloak bag of guts'. But remember, Falstaff has warned: 'It is my intention in writing these memorials to set down *everything*. If that diet of exper-ience proves too rich or strange a meal for some stomachs, then, Eat elsewhere is my advice, and wish you better appetites.'

PATRICK WELLAND enjoys more leisurely writing after a career in Fleet Street. Like Falstaff, he enjoys drinking in the Boar's Head – but the Sussex pub is 50 miles from the site of its namesake.

Alone on a Wide, Wide Sea

DAVID FLEMING

Stirring tales of true-life adventure are, I suspect, most enjoyed by the unadventurous. Those of us content with a quiet and fairly uneventful life take great delight in reading books by those other impossibly intrepid souls who canoe their way up the Amazon, set off with nothing but a rucksack to explore India by train, or march away into the frozen Antarctic wastes dragging a heavy sledge behind them.

Despite never having hoisted a sail (and having no desire to do so), my own particular vicarious pleasure is reading stories by sailors who have made single-handed voyages round the world. A spate of such books appeared in the late Sixties and early Seventies, most of them by British adventurers who, having seen Everest conquered and the Poles reached, turned instinctively to the world's great oceans for fresh challenges. Robin Knox-Johnston's *A World of My Own* (1969) is one of the best of these autobiographical accounts.

Prior to Francis Chichester's voyage, and his subsequent account of it in *Gipsy Moth Circles the World* (1967), the attention of sailors had been focused on the transatlantic crossing. Chichester opened up a new field of endeavour in both sailing and literary terms, soon to be followed by Alec Rose, but in their circumnavigations both sailors stopped off at Australia. The single-handed, non-stop circumnavigation of the world had yet to be achieved and this is where Knox-Johnston enters the story. Twenty-nine years old, and an officer in the Merchant Navy, he was also intensely patriotic and anxious that the

Robin Knox-Johnston, *A World of My Own* (1969)
Adlard Coles · Pb · 256pp · £12.99 · ISBN 9781472974402

French, who could boast some superb sailors, should not be the first to succeed. A trophy put up by the *Sunday Times* was an added incentive and the race was on.

Leaving Falmouth on 14 June 1968 in his ketch *Suhaili*, Knox-Johnston headed off into open water to sail the route taken by the great clipper ships of the past. Determined by winds and currents and wholly oceanic, avoiding man-made canals, it took him south through the Atlantic, past the tip of Africa and on into the Southern Ocean – arguably the most frightening, desolate and lonely place on Earth where vast waters roar unimpeded round the foot of the world. Once past Australia, he headed for the notoriously stormy Cape Horn before turning north-east and into the Atlantic. He was to sail more than 30,000 nautical miles and spend 313 days alone at sea.

Knox-Johnston is the ideal travel companion for the armchair sailor. With clarity, good humour and modesty he takes us through an extraordinary series of adventures and describes in fascinating detail the daily routine of a traveller alone at sea. As with any book

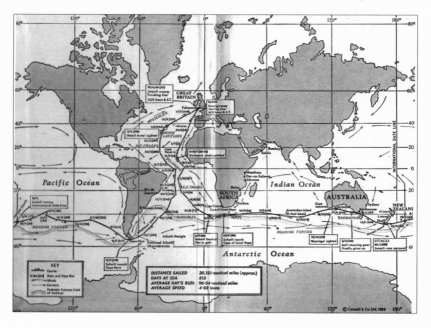

about sailing *A World of My Own* contains technical details to do with the raising and lowering of sails and craft maintenance, but the general reader should not be put off. I can't tell the difference between a swivel snap shackle and a wire splicing spike, and I don't know what it means to whip 'the thimble in the port storm jib sheet eye' or how serious it is to have a 'mass of sail in the oggin'. But it doesn't matter. There's a kind of poetry in this welter of detail that adds to the reading experience, and eventually even the most determined landlubber will pick up some knowledge about the intricacies of self-steering gear or how to use a sextant.

As I read I soon came to realize that courage is not the only quality needed to complete such a voyage. Self-reliance and practical skills are just as important. Constantly making, mending and improvising, you need the skills not just of a sailor, but those of a joiner, metal worker, navigator, radio mechanic, cook, barber and, if you are unlucky, doctor and dentist too. In one of his journal entries he writes:

> After four gales my hands are worn and cut about badly and I am aware of my fingers on account of the pain from skin tears and broken fingernails. I have bruises all over from being thrown about. My skin itches from constant chafing with wet clothes, and I forget when I last had a proper wash so I feel dirty. I feel altogether mentally and physically exhausted and I've been in the Southern Ocean only a week. It seems years since I gybed to turn east and yet it was only last Tuesday night, not six days, and I have another 150 days of it yet.

The hardships faced by lone sailors make for compelling reading, but the more ordinary aspects of their lives are just as fascinating. What food to take on a round-the-world voyage? Knox-Johnston had to choose stores in some haste. His potatoes and onions soon rotted, and the 1,500 tins loaded on to *Suhaili* were not varied enough, causing him to lose interest in food (unlike Alec Rose, and later Chay Blyth, who both took pleasure in their meals at sea).

The trip was far from plain sailing. As well as rotten onions there were problems early on with the fresh-water tank, radio transmitter and self-steering equipment. And *Suhaili* took quite a bashing in rough seas. There was every reason for him to give up at Australia. But of course he went on – real-life adventure, like history, is written by those who have succeeded.

Not all his time was spent hoisting sails. A voracious reader, he took fifty-two books with him, a mini-library comprising nautical texts and classics of world literature (including two of the longest, *War and Peace* and *Clarissa*) as well as biographical works by the likes of Boswell and Rousseau. A full list is given in the appendix to *A World of My Own*, along with details of all the other stores and equipment necessary for a long ocean voyage. As his stock of unread books declined poetry became more important and he began to memorize works from the *Golden Treasury of English Verse*.

A World of My Own conveys a sense of isolation rarely experienced by today's sailors. Digital communications had yet to be invented and the faulty radio transmitter meant he was out of touch with humanity for months at a time. At one point, somewhere in the South Atlantic, he notes:

> Memories of home seem like a dream now, the only reality is my small cabin and the endless empty sea around it. I no longer get excited thinking of home; I mentally shrug the thought of it all off just as I would the memory of the plot in a book. It's nice to think about, but it does not really exist.

Like other single-handed sailors he relied on the natural world for company, particularly on seabirds such as the albatross and storm petrels encountered in waters far from land. He welcomed visits from dolphins, but the appearance of whales made him apprehensive – they could so easily have caused him to capsize. And though appreciative of nature, the ever-practical Knox-Johnston was not averse to shooting a shark when one was persistently circling the boat and so preventing him from getting into the water to make emergency repairs to a leaking hull.

As I read on I find myself pausing to picture *Suhaili* pitching and tossing in wild seas as night falls and the wind blows stronger. In my mind's eye I see cold dawn waves breaking over the boat and filling every nook and cranny with icy waters fresh from the glacial south; and I picture the sparkling blue ocean at the Equator as the boat turns northwards, heading for home on favourable winds. Knox-Johnston's book is not only a first-hand record of a significant chapter in the history of human fortitude, it's a source of inspiration that is guaranteed to raise your spirits.

Though dreaming of the sea, DAVID FLEMING will be confining his nautical adventures to the local boating pond – if he can find someone to do the rowing.

Slightly Foxed also circumnavigates the globe each quarter, travelling to:

ALGERIA · ANGUILLA · ARGENTINA · AUSTRALIA · AUSTRIA · BAHRAIN · BELGIUM
BERMUDA · BOTSWANA · BRAZIL · BULGARIA · CANADA · CHILE · CHINA
COLOMBIA · COSTA RICA · CROATIA · CYPRUS · CZECH REPUBLIC · DENMARK
EGYPT · ESTONIA · ETHIOPIA · FINLAND · FRANCE · GAMBIA · GERMANY
GIBRALTAR · GREECE · GUYANA · HONDURAS · HONG KONG · HUNGARY
ICELAND · INDIA · INDONESIA · IRELAND · ISRAEL · ITALY · JAPAN · JORDAN
KENYA · KUWAIT · LATVIA · LITHUANIA · LUXEMBOURG · MALAYSIA · MALTA
MARTINIQUE · MAURITIUS · MEXICO · MOLDOVA · MONACO · THE NETHERLANDS
NEW ZEALAND · NORWAY · OMAN · PAKISTAN · THE PHILIPPINES · POLAND
PORTUGAL · PUERTO RICO · ROMANIA · RUSSIA · SAMOA · SERBIA · SINGAPORE
SLOVAKIA · SLOVENIA · SOUTH AFRICA · SOUTH KOREA · SPAIN · SRI LANKA
SWEDEN · SWITZERLAND · TAIWAN · TANZANIA · THAILAND · TRINIDAD & TOBAGO
TURKEY · UKRAINE · UAE · USA · URUGUAY · VIETNAM · YEMEN · ZIMBABWE

Out of the Shadows

ANN KENNEDY SMITH

Take two sisters, Alice and Flora Mayor, identical twins born into a comfortable upper-middle-class family in Surrey in 1872. Their clergyman father was also a professor of classical literature at King's College, London, and their mother Jessie a talented musician and linguist. As members of a Victorian clerical family, the girls had certain duties ('Church as depressing as usual. 2 and a half people there,' young Flora wrote in her diary), but mostly they and their two older brothers had tremendous fun: performing amateur theatricals, skating and playing tennis, singing, writing stories, going to the theatre, and always, always reading: Jane Austen, the Brontë sisters and Mrs Gaskell.

Some of their parents' intellectual interests must have rubbed off though, because at 20, Flora decided to study history at Newnham College, Cambridge. She hated to leave Alice behind, but the sisters wrote to each other every day, Flora's letters bursting with news of boating on the river, late-night cocoa parties, debating and drama. A college photograph of her shows a dark-haired young woman with laughing eyes ('Miss Dant said I'd got a great deal of fun about me'). Alice remained quietly at home, sketching and practising her music, while Flora was having all sorts of new adventures. 'The bicycle is fascinating,' she told Alice, 'it's much easier than skating – not so tiring. Mounting is a trial and one must have knickerbockers for it.'

In the late 1980s, almost a century after Flora, I became a postgraduate student at Cambridge and bought a second-hand bicycle

F. M. Mayor, *The Rector's Daughter* (1924)
Persephone · Pb · 336pp · £14 · ISBN 9781910263303

during my first week. Cycling to the university library every day – in jeans rather than knickerbockers – gave me a delicious sense of freedom. I found a battered green-spined Virago paperback of Flora's novel *The Rector's Daughter* on a market stall and fell in love with it, but I didn't know much about its author. Tidying my bookshelves recently, I rediscovered my student novel collection, and decided to find out more about her.

Growing up, the Mayor twins were close to 'the Aunts', their father's seven unmarried sisters who lived together in Hampstead. All were energetic, cultivated and useful women, but Flora was determined not to be like them or the sister whom she so closely resembled. After four years at Cambridge, she decided to go on the stage, but it wasn't the glamorous life she'd envisaged. With mostly non-speaking parts, little money and endless provincial tours, her health began to suffer. Her ambitions to be a writer seemed to be equally ill-starred. When her collection of stories, *Mrs Hammond's Children*, was published under her stage name 'Mary Strafford' in 1901, the critics were decidedly lukewarm.

So there would be no standing ovation for Flora/Mary, but there was someone waiting in the wings. Ernest Shepherd, a young architect and close friend of one of her brothers, had been in love with her for years. After he was offered a post in the Architectural Survey of India, he travelled to Flora's cheap lodgings in Macclesfield to propose. She said yes, rather to her own surprise. 'Being kissed is so odd,' she told Alice. Ernest left for India, and six months of letters followed, discussing the date of their wedding and their plans for the future.

When the telegram came with the devastating news that Ernest had died of malaria, Flora broke down. At 32, her dreams of a life as an actress and as a cherished wife and mother were over. She poured her feelings into a 'Grief Journal' that she signed Flora Shepherd, the name she would now never have. Writing – and Alice's loving care – were to save her.

Flora's masterpiece, *The Rector's Daughter*, was published under the authorship of F. M. Mayor by the Hogarth Press in 1924. It's a short, quietly humorous and deeply perceptive novel that's as good as anything George Eliot ever wrote. Set in the fictional village of Dedmayne, 'on the way to nowhere' in the eastern counties, most of the action, such as it is, takes place at the Rectory, where the clocks seem to have stopped around 1895. The Rector, Canon Jocelyn, is an octogenarian clergyman whose dignified bearing and 'severe, satirical, and melancholy' eyes make him a striking figure. By contrast, his 35-year-old daughter Mary is described as 'a decline'.

> Her uninteresting hair, dragged severely back, displayed a forehead lined too early. Her complexion was a dullish hue, not much lighter than her hair. She had her father's beautiful eyes, and hid them with glasses.

Dowdy Mary Jocelyn seems nothing like vivacious Flora Mayor, but they have a similar intellectual heritage. 'Books streamed everywhere, all over the house, even up the attic stairs' of the Rectory, but 'not more than three Miltons, because of undesirable views on kings, liberty and divorce'. Canon Jocelyn has a sharp, inquiring mind but his daughter is a puzzle to him, and he fails to grasp her aching need for love. For a time, her older, disabled sister Ruth provides this, but after she dies, only Cook ('a working woman of sixty-three') shows Mary any affection. Novels offer her some solace during the long winter months: Trollope, Charlotte M. Yonge and Jane Austen are 'friends so dear and familiar that they peopled her loneliness'.

Mary has a secret that she does not share with her father or Cook: she writes stories and poetry. By chance, she is introduced to the well-connected Brynhilda, whose poet friend Dermott is enthusiastic about Mary's writing. 'I have never known anyone on such intimate terms with toads,' he writes, 'and this, coupled with a passion for Mother Julian of Norwich, indicates a mind I want to know more of.' Mary, daringly, agrees to visit Brynhilda's bohemian London flat and at first enjoys its relaxed atmosphere. 'There was no snapping, fussiness or anxiety. Mary remembered many throes at the Rectory: if the cat took the day off in the woods, if a member of the household was late.' But after a miserable *soirée* among the fashionable literary set ('it was a tribute to Brynhilda that it should come to such a wrong part of London as Kensington'), Mary realizes that she is little more than an object of curiosity to these bright young things, and she returns with relief to decaying Dedmayne. 'On the whole she was happy. She did not question the destiny life brought her. People spoke pityingly of her, but she did not feel she required pity.'

Like a bright-eyed toad in its shadowy habitat, Mary is content to hide herself away. Then Robert Herbert, a middle-aged clergyman from a neighbouring parish, comes to call. Like Canon Jocelyn, he is a well-read Cambridge graduate, and the two men get on famously, discussing the Greek testament and seventeenth-century folios. Mr Herbert and Mary establish a tentative friendship too, but neither is romantically inclined, or so they tell themselves. One wintry day, as they take their usual walk together in the Rectory garden, everything changes.

> The equinoctial wind rushed through the branches of the old elms and roared like the sea. It gave a colour to Mary's cheeks; her eyes dilated and brightened; the spirit that sometimes showed itself in her writings looked forth. Mr Herbert saw her eyes.

It's a charged encounter that neither of them will ever forget, but like the wind that changes direction unexpectedly, things don't go according to plan.

When *The Rector's Daughter* was first published, it was widely praised by critics who traced its lineage to the writers whom Mayor loved: Jane Austen, George Eliot and Elizabeth Gaskell. 'It is like a bitter *Cranford*,' wrote Sylvia Lynd. The public loved it too, and Boots Library had to restrict its lending rules due to the novel's overwhelming popularity. In 1925 *The Rector's Daughter* was shortlisted for the Prix Femina-Vie Heureuse, an annual literary prize in the interwar years for a work 'calculated to reveal to French readers the true spirit and character of England'. E. M. Forster's *A Passage to India* won it that year, but Mayor's consolation prize was an admiring letter Forster wrote to her that begins 'This is Dedmayne, plus better scenery' (he was staying at his unmarried aunt's house on the Isle of Wight at the time). 'Mary begins as ridiculous and ends as dignified,' he told her, 'this seems to me a very great achievement.'

I like to picture the young Flora Mayor in Cambridge, cycling by the river and dreaming of the adventures that lay ahead of her. Life didn't bring the excitement she wanted, but she found a lasting contentment in her writing, and in sharing a home with her twin. Flora died of pneumonia in 1932 at the age of 59; Alice, who cared for her sister and made it possible for her to write, lived until 1960. F. M. Mayor's small output of novels, including *The Third Miss Symons* (1913) and *The Squire's Daughter* (1929), soon fell out of print, but those who read *The Rector's Daughter* never forgot it. In 1941, amidst the London Blitz, the novelist Rosamond Lehmann paid tribute to Mary Jocelyn as 'my favourite character in contemporary fiction', and in 1967 Leonard Woolf described the novel as 'remarkable' in the fourth volume of his autobiography, *Downhill All the Way*. Encouraged by this, Flora's niece Teresa (Lady Rothschild) asked her brother Andreas Mayor to approach Penguin Books, and *The Rector's Daughter* appeared as a Penguin Modern Classic in 1973. It became a Virago Modern Classic in 1987 and has recently been reissued by Persephone Books with a foreword by Alice and Flora's great-niece, Victoria Gray. It seems somehow right that it was Flora Mayor's nephew and niece, remembering their writer aunt, who helped to bring her extraordinary, understated novel out from the shadows.

ANN KENNEDY SMITH is writing a book about Cambridge women. She still lives in the city, and cycles by the river most days.

Not Your Typical Courtier

MICHAEL BARBER

In 1974, following the publication that year of his 'self-portrait', *Another Part of the Wood*, I did a feature on Kenneth Clark for the BBC World Service. This involved interviewing him at his 'set' in Albany, off Piccadilly, the austerity of which was mitigated by what I took to be a small fortune in paintings and miniatures on the walls. In the book Lord Clark, as he became, described his life (1903–83) as 'one long, harmless confidence trick', a reference to what he called his freak aptitude, apparent from the age of 9 or 10, for responding authoritatively to works of art.

He profited from this, he told me, because most English people didn't 'give a blow about art' and considered it sissy. So when they met someone who could speak with confidence and enthusiasm about paintings and sculpture, they were prepared to listen – 'to save themselves trouble'.

There speaks a highbrow, I remember thinking. And with his domed forehead Clark, known as 'K' to his friends, certainly looked the part. But as I subsequently learnt from James Stourton's superb biography, *Kenneth Clark: Life, Art and Civilisation* (2016), no one since Ruskin had tried harder to forge a bond between the artist and the man in the street. In Clark's own words, 'art is not the prerogative of nobs and snobs, but the right of every man'. Before he became a household name with his BBC series *Civilisation*, he had already

---

Kenneth Clark's *Another Part of the Wood* (1974) and James Stourton's *Kenneth Clark: Life, Art and Civilisation* (2016) are both out of print, but we can obtain second-hand copies.

made, or contributed to, more than sixty television programmes.

One of Clark's Scottish ancestors invented the cotton spinney, a revolutionary device that ensured that his descendants need never lift a finger. Hence this urbane reflection: 'My parents belonged to a section of society known as "the idle rich", and although, in that golden age, many people were richer, there can have been few who were idler' – or, as a couple, so different in temperament. His father was a raffish Edwardian playboy with a luxuriant walrus moustache, who drank gallons of champagne and whisky and broke the bank at Monte Carlo. Clark lets him off pretty lightly, though it's clear that in his cups he could be a dreadful embarrassment. His mother, from a modest Quaker background, was prim and undemonstrative. Only on her deathbed did she reveal how much she loved her son. Neither parent seems to have experienced what Clark calls 'our poor old friend, "pure aesthetic sensation"', though he shared his father's devotion to billiards: 'Nothing else absorbs and concentrates my faculties to the same extent.'

Clark's Oxford mentor, the charismatic don Maurice Bowra, said he was brought up 'with a callousness which only the rich dare to show their children'. An only child, he was not exactly ill-treated, except perhaps at Winchester during the Great War, but at an early age he developed what Henry Moore called a 'glass screen' that people found daunting. Clark said this sprang from his chilly boyhood, and the fear and inexperience that resulted, which was why he acknowledged such a debt to Bowra, who he said had the strongest influence on his life.

Bowra, wrote Clark, 'said all the dreadful things one was longing to hear, and said them as if they were obvious to any decent man . . . My priggish fears and inhibitions were blown to smithereens.' That Bowra should have taken him up was especially noteworthy because Clark, unlike most of the don's other protégés, 'never felt the slightest inclination to homosexuality', which Bowra regarded as the natural condition of an intelligent man. Women would always mean more to Clark than men. He had numerous affairs – 'silly fits' he called them – and for many years kept a flat in Mayfair for trysts.

Clark acknowledged two other mentors, Charles Bell and Bernard Berenson. Bell, the Keeper of Fine Art at the Ashmolean, made him study the museum's trove of drawings by Michelangelo and Raphael, the beginning of his education in art, 'as opposed to looking at pictures in a dilettanteish way'. His debt to Berenson, the sage of I Tatti, under whom he worked for two years in Italy, he summed up as 'difficult to describe and impossible to repay'. Recognizing a kindred spirit, Berenson invited Clark to serve a sort of apprenticeship in 'conoscing', his term for connoisseurship, thus establishing a bond that would last for almost forty years.

Berenson was an autocrat, but Clark, by now a very rich young man, was not your typical courtier. He would defer to Berenson on Art, but not on Life. In 1927 he annoyed his patron by getting married instead of having lots of affairs (sexual gossip rivalled art as a staple of conversation at I Tatti). And by the time he left he was aware that Berenson 'was perched on the pinnacle of a mountain of corruption', a reference to the profitable collusion between dealers like Duveen and experts like Berenson during the heyday of American collecting.

Clark's narrative, which closes in 1939 (he later wrote a sequel, *The Other Half*, published in 1977), is punctuated by a series of disarmingly frank asides. 'I am by nature exceptionally mean,' he says at one point. He also reveals that Berenson's mistress, Nicky Mariano, found him 'rather standoffish and cutting in his remarks, also not free from conceit in one so young'. She was not alone in thinking this, admits Clark. Her other great complaint was that he lacked a sense of humour, a proposition which, he says, the reader must judge for himself.

I couldn't agree less. Clark had a sly, dry wit to match his love of irony and keen eye for detail. His book is full of comic interludes. Nearly fifty years later I can still recall creasing up over his description of Berenson's reaction to some gaudy murals that his wife had unwisely commissioned for his Holy of Holies, the library at I Tatti.

Mr Berenson returned from his journey slightly fatigued, entered his beloved library and immediately fainted. He is said to have fallen flat on the floor, rigid with horror. He was carried to bed, where he remained for a week.

A little later Clark describes how puzzled an Edwardian dowager was by a depiction of the Last Supper, in which the Apostles were sitting round a table with square plates in front of them. '"Look at all those old tramps," she said, in royal accents, "I vonder vot they are playing."'

Clark's precocious aesthetic credentials were established with *The Gothic Revival*, his 'Essay in the History of Taste', which appeared in 1928. But instead of devoting himself to writing, which he described to me as 'the one wholly satisfying activity I have ever undertaken', he bounded up the ladder of preferment as an administrator, replacing Bell at the Ashmolean in 1930 and then three years later becoming Director of the National Gallery at the tender age of 30.

So began, in his own words, the 'Great Clark Boom', during which he and his chic wife Jane became the hottest tickets in town, asked everywhere, and entertaining everyone, including the King and Queen, at their grand house in Portland Place. 'Jane and the K in all around I see,' quipped Bowra. What would he have said about Jane's modish *pièce de résistance*, 'a pair of trousers of emerald green velveteen with a row of large scarlet fly buttons, not up the front, but creeping up behind, along the division between her buttocks'.

Inevitably the Clarks made enemies, including Chips Channon, the socialite and self-styled 'Lord of Hosts', who thought they were bogus. When he asked Jane why they never invited him to dinner, she replied, 'But Chips, we don't know anyone grand enough to invite with you.' It would have been interesting to know what Clark made of Channon, because he relished 'characters', and Chips certainly qualified on that score. Apart from Bowra and Berenson, *Another Part of the Wood* includes lively pen portraits of Joe Duveen, Calouste Gulbenkian, Roger Fry, Philip Sassoon, Sybil Colefax and Edith Wharton, with all of whom he could converse on equal terms.

None of the above considered art sissy, but then they were not the 'supposedly ordinary people' whom the art historian Michael Levey said Clark dedicated himself to winning over. One earnest of this was his sponsorship of contemporary English artists such as Henry Moore, Graham Sutherland, David Piper and Victor Pasmore, none of whom were either well-connected or fashionable (for which read Cubists or Surrealists). All were indebted to his support, which was vindicated in the 1940s when representational and narrative art – the authentic voice of England, so Clark thought – enjoyed a revival.

Strange to relate, Clark thought of himself as a socialist, which may explain the somewhat subversive epiphany he describes on the last page of the book. War has been declared that very morning, and like everyone else he expects there will soon be an air raid. Gazing up towards Piccadilly Circus from Waterloo Place he concludes that it might not be such a bad thing if the 'featureless blocks' he saw were bombed, because 'the social system of which [they] were an emanation was a worn-out monster founded on exploitation. It would be better to start afresh.'

In fact, as he then admits, none of those buildings was bombed. But the war quickened Clark's appetite for public service. On his watch, and despite being emptied of its treasures, the National Gallery, thanks to innovations like the Picture of the Month and Dame Myra Hess's lunchtime concerts, became what Herbert Read called 'a defiant outpost of culture right in the middle of a bombed and shattered metropolis'.

MICHAEL BARBER does not think art is 'sissy', but he can't tell a good picture from a bad one.

Power and the Prince

DEREK PARKER

Recently, the lack of anything worth watching on TV sent me, once again, to the DVD of Visconti's lush 1963 film of Giuseppe Lampedusa's *The Leopard* (1958). If one loves a book, the idea that a film version might be in a different way as satisfactory as the original seems a sort of betrayal. But at the very least I find it impossible to reread the book without Burt Lancaster's Prince Fabrizio, Claudia Cardinale's ravishing Angelica and Alain Delon's handsome, self-regarding Tancredi illustrating the narrative as a most remarkable set of lithographs might.

The author of course provided his own vivid panorama before the film came along, and a reader with no previous sense of the barren, dusty landscape of Sicily and no knowledge of or special interest in the turmoil of Italian society during the Risorgimento does not have to read long before being immersed in the place and time of the novel, and understanding the creaking uncertainty and shock experienced by the society of which Prince Fabrizio is the head.

We meet him and his family first at morning prayers in the vast family palace outside Palermo. Rising from his knees, the Prince wanders into the garden and, as his favourite companion – his Great Dane Bendicò – digs happily in a flowerbed, Fabrizio becomes conscious of a close, sickly atmosphere emanating from the decaying corpse of a Neapolitan soldier who has managed to struggle into the adjacent lemon grove to die. His slow, painful death mirrors the

Giuseppe Tomasi di Lampedusa, *The Leopard* (1958)
Vintage · Pb · 272pp · £9.99 · ISBN 9780099512158

social change that is at the heart of the novel, as the Prince is forced to recognize the inevitable social rise of Sedàra, the uncouth, wily mayor of Donnafugata, where Fabrizio has a summer villa. The mayor, he realizes, has through chicanery become considerably richer than the Prince himself.

The Leopard was the single book written by Giuseppe Tomasi di Lampedusa, the only child of a grandee of Spain, Prince of Lampedusa, Duke of Palma di Montechiaro and Baron of Torretta, with a palace in Palermo. He completed *Il Gattopardo* in 1956, and before his death

the following year saw it rejected by two publishers. Published post-humously it swiftly became a worldwide literary sensation. The English title, *The Leopard*, resonates but isn't quite what Lampedusa meant. The *gattopardo* was a wildcat hunted to extinction in the nineteenth century; the author's reference was clearly to the grandees of Sicilian aristocracy, forced to come to terms with the new Kingdom of Italy which was supported by a greedy, corrupt, unprincipled liberal *bourgeoisie* set on destroying the old Bourbon aristocracy.

The Prince makes the early decision that it will be impossible to fight the social changes which he clearly foresees, and concentrates instead on saving what he can of his depleted finances by the marriage of the beautiful Angelica, daughter of the vulgar mayor, to his wayward nephew Prince Tancredi, who has happily fallen in love with her. There is a wonderful chapter celebrating the courtship of Tancredi and Angelica as they wander through the countless neglected rooms of the palace (like other chapters, so cinematic that it is no surprise that Visconti could not resist it); but the reader is left in no doubt that the marriage, though saving for a time the family's finances, is doomed to be as unsatisfactory as that of the Prince himself, wed to a religious and puritanical wife. He regularly rides off to visit one of the local prostitutes, his expeditions less than satisfactorily excused by the company of the family's priest.

The portrait of Prince Fabrizio is comprehensive in its characterization of a man deeply troubled by the contradictions in which he finds himself enmeshed. His beloved Tancredi becomes a traitorous follower of the invading Garibaldi, and he knows that in encouraging Tancredi's marriage to Angelica he is betraying his own favourite daughter, Concetta, who has always loved the young tearaway. Financially astute, he is also deeply sentimental, devoted to hunting and shooting. Out one day with a companion, he injures a wild rabbit and then picks it up and cradles it:

> the velvety ears were already cold, the vigorous paws contracting in rhythm, still-living symbol of useless flight; the animal had died tortured by anxious hopes of salvation . . . While sympathetic fingers were still stroking that poor snout, the animal gave a last quiver and died; Don Fabrizio and Don Ciccio had had their bit of fun, the former not only the pleasure of killing but also the comfort of compassion.

The book has much to say about the parallel lines of reality and sentiment: Tancredi and his friends come straight from the killing of the battlefield to the drawing-room of the Prince's palace, and there they offer carefully edited anecdotes of blood and thunder to the ladies. There is also much discussion of current Italian politics, with special reference to Sicily's part in any possible solution to the muddle, and it must be admitted that there are lengthy passages which only a very determined reader is likely to read with fascinated interest.

Fabrizio's beloved dog Bendicò, distinguished by a glass eye, plays an essential part in the story – indeed in a letter to a friend the author asserted that he is 'a vitally important character and practically the key to the novel'. The book, indeed, ends twenty-seven years after the Prince's death in a scene where the aged Concetta realizes that an unpleasant smell in her rooms emanates from the skin of Bendicò, turned into a now moth-eaten rug. Thrown out of a window, 'its form recomposed itself for an instant; in the air there seemed to be dancing a quadruped with long whiskers, its right foreleg raised in imprecation. Then all found peace in a heap of livid dust.'

The book's publication caused a tremendous furore in Italy. The author's view was clearly that of the Prince: 'We were the Leopards, the Lions, those who'll take our place will be little jackals, hyenas; and the whole lot of us, Leopards, jackals and sheep, we'll go on thinking ourselves the salt of the earth.' It was not a sentiment to please every reader, and it is not surprising that it irritated the Catholic Church, the Communist Party and the residual nobility of Sicily in equal measure. But within a few years it was recognized as one of the greatest novels of the twentieth century.

DEREK PARKER has returned to England from Sydney, where he enjoyed the company of several subscribers to *Slightly Foxed*.

My Years as a Pony

FRANCES DONNELLY

Between the ages of 8 and 11 I thought I was a pony. I was not alone: my friends were in the grip of a similar delusion. We created fantasy mounts called Daybreak or Nutmeg, then became them. We never ran when we could gallop, at all times slapping our sides for greater verisimilitude. Jumps were constructed and then scrambled over or refused with much rearing and neighing. Fortunately our brothers were still pretending to be Spitfires, so our behaviour, on the whole, passed unremarked.

The intensity of these games was fuelled by the longing for a pony and the knowledge that it wouldn't happen. Even riding lessons were expensive at 7s 6d an hour, though they were essential. How else could you display your riding kit? I had a pair of third-hand jodhpurs, a yellow polo-neck jersey knitted by my long-suffering granny, a check Viyella shirt and a tie printed with horses' heads and restrained by a tie pin embellished with horseshoes. I even owned a hard hat which was excruciatingly uncomfortable: I have a rather large head. How right our dear late Queen was always to commit her safety on horseback to a vintage Hermès headscarf. But other than this and enviously spectating at gymkhanas with a satchel of Marmite sandwiches, the main way of feeding my pony obsession was by borrowing pony books from my local library.

Both Fidra Books (www.fidrabooks.com) and Jane Badger Books (www.janebadgerbooks.co.uk) have reissued pony books by Caroline Akrill, Joanna Canaan, Primrose Cumming, Ruby Ferguson, H. M. Peel, K. M. Peyton and Josephine Pullein-Thompson, among many others.

I cannot convey how important the library was in the 1950s. In my Letts diaries, the same entries are endlessly repeated: 'Went to Church', 'Washed hair' and 'Went to Library', but the greatest of the three was the library. I'd love to be able to say that I sped straight to the Brontë section. In reality my twin literary loves were boarding-school stories and pony books. I still have a huge affection for both. Stories about boarding-school life were formulaic but that's what I loved about them: the signposting was unabashed and the rules clearly laid down. The shy heroine had just joined the Lower Fourth but would soon have a zany best friend to pilot her through the shark-infested waters of St Faith's. Familiar tropes abounded. Unpopular girls, girls who sneaked and wouldn't share their tuck, were called Rhoda or Muriel. Loyalty to your chums was everything. The story had to happen over one term and the story arc would be triumphantly resolved by who won the end-of-term Interhouse Lacrosse Cup. There was often a shocking subplot such as who had stolen the Pet Club subscription money. If it was a Second World War story, suspicion would eventually fall on the unfriendly German teacher, Frau Schmidt, who was often to be seen on the cliffs, signalling frantically to enemy submarines. Clearly, in the event of an invasion, the German High Command needed all the money they could lay their hands on.

I loved pony books with equal intensity. Those by the incomparable Pullein-Thompson sisters, Diana, Christine and Josephine (11 million copies sold worldwide), were first in my heart, closely followed by Ruby M. Ferguson, she of the 'Jill's Gymkhana' books (see *SF* no.58). I knew a serious aspirant rider ought to be studying *The Art of Equitation* by the likes of Colonel 'Jumbo' Chudleigh Fortescue. But what my young self pined for, panted for, were books with thrillingly simple titles like: *I Wanted a Pony* or *Six Ponies* or *Pony Club Team*. These books breathed the warm fug of the stable, describing the duties I longed for, like grooming and keeping my tack in tiptop order, and they allowed me entry into that magical world of gymkhanas and Pony Club camps.

Of course they had their own formulaic tropes. The heroine was invariably not well off, and she'd been bought a decidedly iffy, untrained pony whom a farmer wanted to unload for £15 plus tack. Via kindly friends she would learn schooling and proper pony management. The story would lead inexorably towards triumph at the local gymkhana. But the road there was strewn with embarrassing falls and snooty girls. Muriel's equestrian equivalent (she who would not share her fruitcake) was a Susan or a Fiona whose parents were wealthy but who were nouveaux riches pot-hunters. What this actually meant was that they were constantly buying their daughters expensively trained show ponies, which were summarily sold if Susan or Fiona didn't win a red rosette and a cup in every class she entered.

Both types of book told a rattling good yarn, but while school stories were uncomplicated good fun, pony books had a level of seriousness about them. Their moral message was clear and unequivocal: if you own a pony you have duties and responsibilities. However tired you are, the pony comes first. It needs feeding and watering, and then it must be tucked up in a clean stable with a net of fragrant hay. Furthermore, if you are offered a young, untrained horse your role is to help it fulfill its potential by gentle and patient schooling, not by using a whip and brute force. In all these books there was a great deal of technical riding advice which I drank in. Who else was going to teach me the difference between a standing and a running martingale, information that has served me well throughout my adult life?

Years ago I was fortunate enough to interview Christine Pullein-Thompson when she and her husband moved to a moated former parsonage near Diss in Norfolk, a house full of warmth and animals. She gave me a fascinating insight into the world she and her sisters had known in rural Oxfordshire. Their large shabby house was set in a landscape filled with Majors and Colonels, many of whom, like their own father, had been injured in the First World War. He was reduced to selling that new commodity, the Fridge. To make ends meet their mother wrote pony books under her maiden name of Joanna Canaan. I knew and loved them: among my favourites was *A Pony for Jean*, followed by *Another Pony for Jean* and – you guessed it – *More Ponies for Jean*.

Seated at the kitchen table, Joanna Canaan had written at least one book a year for forty years. She set her daughters an excellent example and that was just as well, because she didn't believe in a traditional education for her girls, though their brother naturally went to Eton. Self-reliance, she taught her daughters, was everything. They listened carefully. Thus by their mid-teens they had not only set up their own riding school but had also joined their mother at the kitchen table. The three teenage sisters started their writing careers with a joint endeavour called *It Began with Picotee*. It was snapped up and published in 1946.

I asked Christine when they'd all learnt to ride. 'Quite late in the day,' she replied, somewhat dryly. 'Up till then we'd simply scrambled on to available ponies and hung on till we fell off. It probably didn't occur to our mother that lessons might be a good thing until we were all lying, concussed, in separate rooms. And as soon as we'd learnt, we wanted to teach other people.'

Psychologists have offered various tedious theories about the attachment of little girls to horses –in particular declaring that they are drawn to those muscular heaving flanks by prepubertal sexual longings. I couldn't possibly comment. But for my generation, the explanation seems so much simpler. We were 1950s girls, still obliged to wear gloves and hats to school and to strive at all times to be lady-like. We were also thought to be in need of the support of a manly arm. Pony books gave the lie to all that by offering us vigorous, admir-able role models, in a sport where men and women could compete equally.

It's gratifying to discover that many of the books I loved are back in print, seventy years later, beautifully presented and published – incontrovertible proof, if any more were needed, of the imaginative power and value of pony books. It's wonderful to know that the books that gave me such pleasure are clearly delighting a new gener-ation of pony-loving little girls all over the world.

FRANCES DONNELLY still lives on the Norfolk/Suffolk border.

The *Slightly Foxed* Crossword No. 14: Answers

Across: 1 GATSBY 4 ADAM BEDE 10 VOLUNTEER 11 REEVE
12 SPARSIT 13 *and 24 down* TEARING HASTE 14 OMEGA
15 CHEERILY 18 AN ADVERB 20 UJIJI 23 AIRSHOW
25 ORLANDO 26 LASTS 27 NAKED HAND 28 ACADEMES
29 READER

Down: 1 GAVESTON 2 TALLAGE 3 BANDSTAND
5 DOROTHEA BROOKE 6 MARIA 7 EZEKIEL 8 ENERGY
9 BESTE-CHETWYNDE 16 ROUTLEDGE 17 DISORDER
19 NERISSA 21 INNYARD 22 DAHLIA 24 *See 13 across*

Bibliography

Coming attractions

IAN THOMSON catches a train to Budapest · PAULINE MELVILLE drops in on Compton Mackenzie · FLORA WATKINS remembers the summer of 1900 · NICK HUNT travels through America's Badlands · POSY FALLOWFIELD longs to belong · JOHN KEAY spends time before the mast · MAGGIE FERGUSSON encounters an unwelcome guest · CHRISTIAN TYLER takes up fly-fishing · URSULA BUCHAN meets a literary gardener

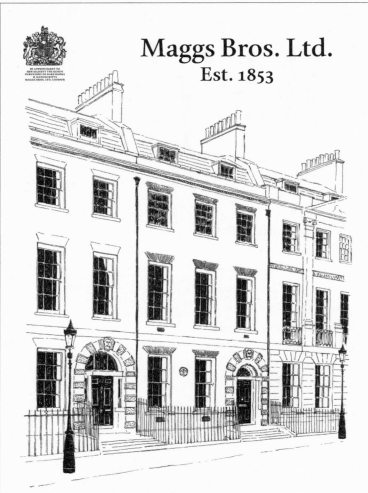

Maggs Bros. Ltd.
Est. 1853

BY APPOINTMENT TO
HER MAJESTY THE QUEEN
PURVEYORS OF RARE BOOKS
& MANUSCRIPTS
MAGGS BROS. LTD. LONDON

RARE BOOKS AND MANUSCRIPTS

48 Bedford Square & 46 Curzon Street
+44 (0)207 493 7160 • ENQUIRIES@MAGGS.COM
WWW.MAGGS.COM